Complete English Grammar Workbook for Adult Beginners

Write and Speak English in 30 Days!

Explore to Win

Table of Contents

🎁 Access Your Exclusive Free Bonuses!

Congratulations on the purchase of your new book by Explore To Win!

As a thank you, we are thrilled to offer you incredible bonuses of significant value. To access these valuable resources, simply scan the QR code below.

English Flashcards Combo + Audiobook & More

Introduction

"Language is the road map of a culture. It tells you where its people come from and where they are going."

- Rita Mae Brown

Do you want to learn English as an adult but aren't sure where to start? Do all the language's rules make you feel overwhelmed? Are you tired of feeling left out of conversations because you don't speak English? If this describes you, you've come to the right place!

Learn English Grammar Workbook for Adult Beginners: Write and Speak English in 30 Days! is the perfect book for taking you from beginner to fluent in just one month! This is more than just another English grammar book; it is a comprehensive guide to achieving fluency quickly and effectively, designed specifically for ESL students.

Our easy-to-use workbook will help you quickly improve your listening, speaking, reading, and writing skills. Learning a new language can be difficult, especially when it comes to understanding the complex rules of English grammar. But don't worry; this workbook will assist you every step of the way.

Being able to communicate effectively in English, can open a whole new world of opportunities, ranging from career advancement to travel and cultural experiences. With this in mind, we created this workbook to help you, as an adult beginner, become conversational in the English language. Our goal is to make the learning process as simple, enjoyable, and effective as possible so that you can confidently begin speaking and writing in English.

We all know that the English language is difficult. Especially, English grammar can be a difficult subject to understand fully. But don't worry, we've got you covered! This workbook is a comprehensive guide to English grammar, covering topics ranging from nouns, verbs, and adjectives to conditionals, reported speech, and phrasal verbs. We believe that with the right approach and direction, anyone can learn to speak English fluently. That is why we created this workbook for adult beginners. Our goal is to provide you with clear explanations, practical examples, and engaging exercises that will help you in understanding and applying the language concepts that you must know.

Each chapter is designed to build on the one before it, allowing you to gradually improve your skills and knowledge.

We believe that the key to understanding English grammar is practice. As a result, we've included a wide range of exercises in this workbook to help you reinforce your learning. Each exercise is carefully designed to assess your understanding of the concepts covered in the chapter, allowing you to identify areas where you need to improve.

We accept that learning grammar can be a dry and monotonous experience, which is why we've included a lot of fun and engaging elements in this workbook. Each chapter includes inspirational quotes to keep you motivated!

The workbook is divided into three parts, each covering a different aspect of English grammar. Book One covers the fundamentals of English grammar, including nouns, verbs, adjectives, and prepositions. This book is ideal for beginners who are just learning English or need a refresher on the fundamentals.

The authors aren't just fluent in English, but also have considerable experience teaching the language to beginners, which differentiates this book from other English language learning resources. They apply this knowledge to provide practical guidance and support as you work toward your language goals.

By the end of this workbook, you will have a thorough understanding of English grammar and be able to confidently apply it in your writing and speaking. **What's more, the best part? You'll have accomplished everything in just 30 days!** That's right, you can learn English grammar quickly and effectively with our workbook without sacrificing quality.

So, what are you waiting for? Take the first step toward becoming conversational in English today and join the millions of people who have already learned to speak English fluently all over the world with this book designed specifically for ESL students. Let us begin together and make English learning fun!

Chapter 1: Introduction to English Grammar

"Grammar is not a set of rules to be memorized. It's a tool to be used to convey meaning."

\- Richard Nordquist

Hello and welcome to the fascinating world of English grammar! Before we get into the nitty-gritty details, let's first define grammar and why it's so important.

Consider grammar to be the backbone of the English language. Grammar, like a strong backbone, supports your ability to communicate effectively in English. Your sentences would be like a Jenga tower without a solid foundation - unstable and prone to collapsing at any time. But don't worry! In this chapter, we'll help you lay a solid foundation and master the fundamentals of English grammar.

Don't worry, we're not going to bore you with extreme rules and exceptions. Instead, we'll use real-life examples you can relate to and apply in your daily conversations. By the end of this chapter, you'll be well on your way to confidently and effectively expressing yourself in English.

So, let's get started and have some grammar fun!

Basic Components of Speech

Let's start exploring the fundamental concepts of English grammar - the building blocks of every sentence, also known as the "parts of speech". Nouns, verbs, adjectives, adverbs, pronouns, prepositions, conjunctions, and interjections will be covered.

Nouns:

First, there are nouns. These are the names of people, places, things, and ideas - basically anything! Consider nouns to be the foundation of any sentence; without them, you wouldn't be able to say much. "Cat," "dog," "table," "chair," "teacher," "school," and "love" are all nouns.

Look for words that can be used with articles like "*a*," "*an*," or "*the*" to identify a noun. "A dog," "an idea," and "the city," for example, are all noun phrases.

Verbs:

Then there are **verbs,** which are the action words that give your sentence life. Verbs describe what the subject does or is. Every sentence requires a verb, whether it is about running, eating, or simply existing.

For Example:

"I am singing a song."

In this sentence, *"singing"* is the verb because it describes the action that "I" am doing.

So, to decide if a word is a verb, ask yourself, "Does it describe an action or a state of being?" If you answered yes, it's most likely a verb!

Adjectives:

Then there are **adjectives,** which are flashy, descriptive words that add color to your sentences. They add details and help your reader understand what you're saying. So, instead of saying, 'the dog ran,' you could say, 'the fluffy, brown dog ran happily'.

They help deliver extra details about a noun or pronoun's size, shape, color, age, or any other characteristic. As an example:

- The _large_ dog followed the _small_ cat.
- She attended the party in a _red_ dress.
- I noticed an _old_ gentleman walking slowly down the street.

The adjectives "large," "small," "red," and "old" in these sentences all provide additional information about the nouns they describe. Adjectives are essential parts of speech because they allow us to write more imaginative and descriptive sentences.

Adverbs:

Adverbs are descriptive words for verbs, adjectives, or other adverbs. They frequently end in _"-ly"_ and can provide additional information about how an action is performed, how something looks or feels, or how frequently something occurs. In the sentence "She sings _beautifully_," for example, the word "_beautifully_" is an adverb that describes how she sings.

Here are some more examples:

- He spoke _clearly._
- She moved _slowly._
- They are playing _happily._

Pronouns:

A pronoun is a word that stands in for a noun. It prevents us from repeatedly using the same noun in a sentence or paragraph. A pronoun can refer to a person, place, thing, or idea.

Instead of saying "John went to John's house and John's dog barked at John," we can say, "John went to his house and his dog barked at him."

Here are some common pronouns in English:

- I
- you
- he
- she
- it
- we
- they
- me
- him
- her
- us
- them

Personal pronouns (I, you, he, she, etc.), possessive pronouns (mine, yours, his, hers, etc.), and demonstrative pronouns are the three types of pronouns (this, that, these, those).

Correctly using pronouns is essential for clear and concise communication in English.

Prepositions:

Prepositions are words in a sentence that show the relationship between a noun or pronoun and other words. They typically describe the location or direction of an action, person, or thing. "The dog is under the table," or "I'm going to work" for example. The prepositions "on" and "to" in these sentences indicate the position and direction of the dog and the person.

"In," "on," "at," "under," "over," "behind," "before," "after," "with," "without," "from," "to," and "between" are some common prepositions. Understanding prepositions is essential for improving the descriptive and precise nature of your sentences.

Conjunctions:

Conjunctions are words in a sentence that connect words, phrases, or clauses. They help in demonstrating the relationship between the various parts of a sentence. In English, common conjunctions include "and" "or" "but" "so" "yet" and "for."

Here are some examples using conjunctions:

- I love eating sushi and ramen ("and" connects two nouns)

- You can play games or workout ("or" connects two options)
- He is tired, but he must go to work. ("But" connects two opposing ideas)
- He studied hard, so he got a good grade at English. ("So" connects two cause and effect statements)

Interjection:

Words or phrases used to express strong emotions or reactions are known as interjections. They are usually short and end with an exclamation point, such as *"Wow!"* or *"Ouch!"*

Interjections are not usually required grammatically in a sentence, but they can add emphasis or convey a specific tone or feeling. For example, if you want to express surprise, you could say *"Wow!"* or *"Oh my goodness!"* You could use the interjection *"Ouch!"* to express pain.

Overall, interjections are a fun and expressive part of the English language because they allow speakers to convey strong emotions and reactions in just one word or phrase.

Congrats! You now understand the fundamental components of English speech. From nouns and verbs to adjectives, adverbs, pronouns, prepositions, conjunctions, and interjections, you're well on your way to becoming a grammatically correct sentence construction expert.

We've made this handy chart with examples of each part of speech to help you remember everything you've learned. Keep it nearby and use it as a reminder whenever you need it. With time and practice, you'll be able to use these parts of speech with confidence and ease.

Part of Speech	Explanation	Example
Noun	A person, a place, a thing, or idea	Car, house, t-shirt, ice cream, dog, pizza…
Verb	a course of action or a state of being	Run, write, speak, read, sing, jump…
Adjective	Describes a noun or a pronoun	Big, small, tall, short, old, young, fast, slow…
Adverb	explains a verb, an adjective, or another adverb	Quickly, slowly, clearly, certainly, lovely…
Pronoun	Replaces a noun	I, you, we, they, he, she, it
Preposition	demonstrates how a noun or pronoun is related to other words in a sentence.	In, on, at, under, between, in front of…
Conjunction	Connects sentences, clauses, or words.	But, however, and, so, as…
Interjection	A word or phrase used to express intense feelings.	Wow! Oh my god! Hurray! Ugh…

Simple Sentence Construction

Prepare to construct your own sentences like a pro! In this section, we will demonstrate how to construct simple sentences in English. It's not about memorizing boring rules; instead, we'll teach you through real-life examples and enjoyable activities!

First and foremost, let's discuss **subject-verb agreement**. This simply means that the subject (who or what the sentence is about) and verb (action or state of being) must be the same. You wouldn't say "The cat is running," for example, because "cat" is singular and "are" is plural. "The cat is running," you'd say instead, with "is" being the correct singular form of the verb.

Let's get started with basic sentence structures. *Subject-verb-object (SVO)* and *subject-verb-complement (SVC)* are the most common structures (SVC). The subject performs the action on the object in an SVO sentence. "John (subject) eats (verb) pizza (object)" for example. A linking verb connects the subject to a complement (a word that completes the meaning of the sentence) in an SVC sentence. "She (subject) is (linking verb) happy (complement)" for example.

But enough with the boring stuff! Let's put this knowledge to use with some real-life examples. Assume you're at a party and want to talk to someone new. "Hello, my name is John (subject), and I (subject) enjoy (verb) playing basketball. (object)" See how simple that was? "I (subject) am (verb) a dancer (complement)," for example. You could even add some adjectives to describe yourself, such as "I (subject) am (verb) a passionate (adjective) salsa (object) dancer (complement)."

Here is a chart to help you remember it easily!

Sentence Structure	Example
Subject-Verb	The dog barks.
Subject-Verb-Object	She reads a book.
Subject-Verb-Complement	He is a doctor.

A *subject* is the person, place, or thing that is performing or being described. In a sentence, a verb is the action or state of being. An object is the person, place, or thing that receives the verb's action. A complement is a phrase or word that describes the subject or object.

In the first example, the subject is "the dog," the verb is "barks," and there is no object or complement.

"She" is the subject in the second example, "reads" is the verb, and "a book" is the object.

"He" is the subject in the third example, "is" is the verb, and "a doctor" is the complement.

Key Takeaways

- Grammar is an important tool for communicating meaning in the English language.
- Sentences are made up of nouns, verbs, adjectives, adverbs, pronouns, prepositions, conjunctions, and interjections.
- Nouns are the names we give to people, places, things, and ideas.
- Verbs are descriptive action words that describe what the subject does or is.
- Adjectives add flavor to sentences by describing the properties of nouns or pronouns.
- Adverbs are descriptive words that add to the meaning of verbs, adjectives, or other adverbs.
- Pronouns serve as noun substitutes, preventing repetition.
- Prepositions demonstrate the connection between a noun or pronoun and other words.
- Conjunctions join words, phrases, and clauses together to form longer sentences.
- Interjections are used to convey strong feelings or emotions.

Now it's time to put your newfound language skills to the test! Don't worry, this isn't your average boring test with tedious questions and long explanations. This is your chance to demonstrate what you've learned in a fun and interactive way. So take a deep breath, relax, and let's begin!

Basic Building Blocks: Put Your Understanding of Simple Sentence Construction to the Test

1) Which of the following is a noun?

a) run

b) come

c) cat

d) quickly

2) Which of the following is a verb?

a) car

b) sleep

c) big

d) in

3) Which of the following is an adjective?

a) dance

b) quickly

c) table

d) happy

4) Which of the following is an adverb?

a) run

b) jump

c) today

d) dog

5) Which of the following is a pronoun?

a) apple

b) she

c) sing

d) tall

6) Which of the following is a preposition?

a) happy

b) under

c) walk

d) tree

7) Which of the following is a conjunction?

a) run

b) and

c) happy

d) quickly

8) Which of the following is an interjection?

a) run

b) wow

c) sleep

d) small

9) Choose the correct verb to complete the sentence: She _____ to school every day.

a) walk

b) walks

c) walked

d) walking

10) Choose the correct adjective to complete the sentence: The _____ car is green.

a) fast

b) quickly

c) happy

d) run

11) Choose the correct adverb to complete the sentence: She sings _____.

a) in

b) well

c) fast

d) dog

12) Choose the correct pronoun to complete the sentence: _____ is my friend.

a) Table

b) She

c) Dance

d) Tall

13) Choose the correct preposition to complete the sentence: The book is _____ the table.

a) happy

b) between

c) walk

d) on

14) Choose the correct conjunction to complete the sentence: I like pizza _____ I don't like mushrooms.

a) run

b) but

c) or

d) quickly

15) Choose the correct interjection to complete the sentence: _____!
That's awesome, George!

a) run

b) wow

c) sleep

d) small

Answer Key:

1)c, 2)b, 3)d, 4)c, 5)b, 6)b, 7)b, 8)b, 9)b, 10)a, 11)b, 12)b, 13)b, 14)b, 15)b

Congratulations! You've taken the first step toward becoming fluent in English. You've already started down the road to success by understanding the fundamentals of English grammar. In the next chapter, we'll dive deeper into the world of verb tenses and learn how to confidently express ourselves in the present tense. Remember that each new concept you learn adds to your language arsenal, allowing you to communicate more effectively with others. So let us keep going and explore the exciting possibilities that await us in the world of English grammar.

Chapter 2: Living in The Present Tense

"The present moment is filled with joy and happiness. If you are attentive, you will see it."

- Thich Nhat Hanh

Hello, and welcome back! In this chapter, we will look at the present tense, which is all about being present in the moment. It's about what we do every day, what we're doing right now, and what we've been doing for a while. Now let's get started and learn about the present perfect, present progressive/continuous, and simple present tenses.

The simple present tense comes first. This is the tense we use to describe things we do on a regular or habitual basis. "I drink coffee every morning," for example, or "She walks her dog every evening." It's a straightforward and simple tense, but it's an excellent way to describe your daily routines and habits.

The following tense is the present continuous tense. For ongoing events, use the present continuous tense. You can use expressions like "They're playing video games right now" or "I'm writing this chapter right now" are examples. It is a great way to convey what you are doing right now, while being a little trickier to use than the standard present tense.

The last tense is present perfect. This tense is used to describe actions that began in the past but are still now taking place. For instance, "She has worked for them since high school," or "I have resided in this city for more than 20 years." It is a powerful tense to employ when you need to describe how long you have been doing something.

Now, let us get into detail!

The Present Simple Tense

One of the most widely used verb tenses in English is the simple present tense. It's used to describe things that are now occurring or frequent occurrences. For instance, "He swims every day" or "I play video games."

When the subject is a third-person singular, we typically only add an "s" to the end of the verb to create the simple present tense (he, she, it). For instance, "She eats cereal in the morning" or "He plays the piano." However, we use the base form of the verb when the subject is in the first or second person singular or in the plural (we, you, they). For instance, "I enjoy to swim" or "We study English."

Here is a chart to help you remember the correct form:

Pronouns	Positive Form	Negative Form	Question Form
I/You/We/They	I/you/We/They play	I/You/We/They Do not play.	Do I/You/We/They play?

He/She/It	He/She/It play**s**	He/She/It does not play	Does He/She/It play?
Other pronouns or nouns	[Name] play**s**	[Name] does not play	Does [Name] play?

Note: The word "play" is used as an example. Any verb can be used in its place. In the present simple tense, always place the auxiliary verb "do" before the subject when using question forms. In these situations, the 's' is linked to the "do." Just like in negative and question forms.

Examples:

✓ <u>Does</u> Emily clean her room?
✓ She <u>does not</u> clean her room.

Moreover, the words "do" and "not" are often combined to create the word <u>"don't"</u> when they are used together. For example, we can say, "I don't like tea" instead of "I do not like tea." Knowing this contraction will be helpful because it is frequently used in both written and spoken English.

The simple present tense is frequently employed with many verbs, including "eat," "drink," "walk," "run," "speak," and "learn." These verbs are used mostly to indicate routine behaviors or facts.

The simple present tense is used in the following examples of sentences:

- I eat pizza every day.
- She studies medicine.
- We watch movies on the weekends.
- They work from home.
- He works at a hair salon.
- John helps her father.

If you wish to speak and write English well, you should be able to understand the simple present tense, which is an important component of English grammar. However, it is quite "simple" as you can see, and I am sure you will get the hang of it very quickly!

The Present Progressive/Continuous Tense

The present continuous tense is used to describe current events, usually in the present moment. It is formed by using the present tense of the verb "to be," followed by the verb's present participle (ending in "-ing"). "I'm studying right now," for example.

Usage:

The present continuous tense is used to describe events that are taking place right now or in the near future. It is frequently used to refer to ongoing or incomplete actions, as well as to indicate that they are temporary. "She is currently working on a project," for example.

Examples:

Here are some examples of the present continuous/progressive tense:

- ✓ I'm currently working on a book.
- ✓ She is singing a song at the talent show.
- ✓ They are preparing dinner.
- ✓ Enes is working.

Here is a chart to illustrate:

Positive Form	Negative Form	Question Form
I am swimming	I am not swimming	Am I swimming?
You are reading	You are not (aren't) reading	Are you reading?
He/She/It is waiting	He/She/It is not (isn't) waiting	Is He/She/It waiting?
We/They are jumping	We/They are not (aren't) jumping	Are They/We jumping?

Note: Remember that when "do" is used in the negative or question forms, the "s" is attached to the auxiliary verb rather than the verb itself. "He does not play," for example, becomes "He is not playing" in the present continuous tense. In the same way, "Does he play?" becomes "Is he playing?" in the present continuous tense.

Present Perfect Tense

The present perfect tense describes actions that began in the past and continue to the present, as well as actions that were completed in the past but have a connection to the present. In other words, it refers to a past event that has some relevance to the present.

Present perfect tense examples:

- I've already eaten breakfast.

The speaker is referring to a past action (eating breakfast) that has a connection to the present (it's still morning) in this example.

- She has spent the last five years in New York.

This sentence refers to a past action (she moved to New York five years ago) that is still relevant in the present (she still lives there).

- They had completed their homework.

This sentence denotes a completed action in the past (completing homework) with a link to the present (they are now free to do something else).

To create the present perfect tense, combine the auxiliary verb "have" (or "has" for third-person singular subjects) and the main verb's past participle. The past participle is formed by adding "ed" to regular verbs or by using the irregular verb's third form.

Forming the present perfect tense:

- I have studied for the exam.

"Studied" is the past participle of "study" in this example.

- She has cooked dinner for us.

"Cooked" is the past participle of "cook" in this example.

- They've seen the film twice.

"Seen" is the past participle of "see" in this example.

The present perfect tense is frequently used with the verbs "have," "be," "go," "do," "see," "eat," "drink," and "meet."

It's important to distinguish the present perfect tense from the simple past tense, which is used to describe completed actions in the past that have no connection to the present. Learners can use the two tenses effectively in their communication if they understand the differences between them.

This chart will assist you in correctly forming the present perfect tense. It depicts the subject, the auxiliary verb "have/has," and the verb's third form.

Subject	Have/Has	V3
I, you, we, they	Have	Eaten
He/She/It	Has	Eaten

Let's get started with the infamous irregular verbs. Don't be put off by the name; they're not all that bad. 'What are these second and third forms of the verb?!' you may be wondering. Don't worry, it's not rocket science; I'll explain it to you. In general, irregular verbs are any verb that does not follow the standard pattern of adding 'ed' to make the past tense. (We'll save the second form of the verbs for when we discuss the simple past tense). But for the time being, let's concentrate on the present perfect tense and the elusive third form of the verbs. It may appear that there is a lot to remember but think of it as learning a secret language!

Here's a list of some common irregular verbs, as well as their base form, past tense, and past participle forms:

Base Form	Past tense (V2)	Past Participle (V3)
go	went	gone
be	Was/were	been
do	did	done
have	had	had
eat	ate	eaten
run	ran	run
speak	spoke	spoken

write	wrote	written
see	saw	seen
give	gave	given

And, thankfully, not all verbs are irregular! Most verbs can be converted to their third form by adding '-ed' or '-d' or '-ied' at the end. Here are a couple of examples:

- ✓ Walk > Walked
- ✓ Talk > Talked
- ✓ Play > Played
- ✓ Jump > Jumped
- ✓ Watch > Watched
- ✓ Learn > Learned/Learnt
- ✓ Like > Liked
- ✓ Cook > Cooked
- ✓ Help > Helped
- ✓ Want > Wanted

As you can see, the third form of these verbs is created simply by adding "-ed" to the end of the base form.

Key Takeaways

1. **Present Simple Tense**
   - Used to describe routine behaviors or general truths.
   - When the subject is singular, add 's' or 'es' to the base form of the verb.
   - When the subject is plural or in the first person, the base form of the verb is used (I, we, you, they).
   - The auxiliary verb "do" or "does" is used to form negatives and questions.
   - "I study every day," for example. "She doesn't eat apples," "Do you like coffee?"

2. **Present Continuous Tense**
   - Used to describe actions that are currently taking place or are in the process of taking place.
   - The present participle (base verb + -ing) is used to form the verb.
   - The auxiliary verb "to be" is used in conjunction with the present participle.
   - "I am currently studying," for example. "Is she eating breakfast?" "Are you watching television?"

3. **Present Perfect Tense**
   - Used to describe past actions that have a connection to the present or were completed recently.
   - The present participle (base verb + -ing) is combined with the auxiliary verb "have" or "has".
   - Irregular verbs have a distinct third form.

- "I have studied for three hours," "She has already eaten breakfast," "Have you seen that movie?"

4. **Irregular Verbs**
   - Verbs that do not conform to the standard pattern of adding 'ed' to form the past tense.
   - Have their own distinct forms.
   - "Go/went/gone," "eat/ate/eaten," and "swim/swam/swum" are examples of irregular verbs.

Keep in mind that these are only the fundamentals of these tenses and verbs. You will become more comfortable using the English language in conversation and writing as you practice and gain exposure to it.

You did an excellent job learning the present simple, present continuous, and present perfect tenses, as well as irregular verbs! It's now time to put your knowledge to the test by answering some practice questions. Before you begin, stay hydrated and take a deep breath to calm your nerves. Keep in mind that you have this champion!

Exercises

Circle the correct answer.

1) She _____ to school every day.

a) will walk

b) walk

c) walks

d) walked

2) They _____ a good time at the party at the moment.

a) are having

b) had

c) have

d) having

3) We _____ dinner at the moment.

a) are having

b) has

c) have

d) had

4) He _____ his homework before he goes to bed.

a) did

b) do

c) does

d) doing

5) I _____ the news on TV every night.

a) watch

b) watched

c) watching

d) watches

6) They _____ the movie already when I arrived.

a) had watched

b) have watched

c) watching

d) watch

7) She _____ for that company.

a) works

b) will worked

c) working

d) work

8) He _____ to the gym every Monday.

a) goes

b) went

c) go

d) going

9) They _____ their homework right now.

a) doing

b) do

c) does

d) are doing

10) She _____ to the radio now.

a) listens

b) listening

c) is listening

d) listen

11) They _____ in New York before they moved to California.

a) lived

b) live

c) living

d) have lived

12) He _____ his phone before he leaves.

a) checked

b) check

c) checks

d) checking

Answer Key

1)c, 2)a, 3)a, 4)c, 5)a, 6)b, 7)a, 8)a, 9)d, 10)c, 11)d, 12)c

Chapter 3: Unlocking the Secrets of Past Tense

"The past is a place of reference, not a place of residence; the past is a place of learning, not a place of living."
- Roy T. Bennett.

Hello and welcome! Welcome to Chapter 3, where we'll be discussing the past tense. I know what you're thinking: 'Why do I need to learn past tense? After all, I'm living in the present!' But here's the thing: the past tense is essential for understanding and communicating about events in our lives. Using the past tense allows others to understand the timeline of events and engage with your experiences, whether you're telling a story about your childhood, recounting a memorable event, or simply talking about what you did yesterday. So, prepare to enter the world of the past tense with me!

We'll go over everything from regular past tense verbs to irregular past tense verbs, as well as some common phrases and expressions you'll hear in everyday conversation, in this chapter. Don't worry if you're feeling a little intimidated; we'll take it slowly and I'll even throw in some jokes along the way to keep things interesting. Let's get started!

Simple Past Tense

Hello and welcome to the wonderful world of the simple past tense! In case you missed it, the past tense is all about what has already happened. Consider it a time machine that allows you to go back in time and discuss events that have already occurred.

It's now as simple as pie to use regular verbs in the simple past tense. All you have to do is add '-ed' at the end and you have a past-tense verb! It's similar to magic, except instead of pulling rabbits from hats, you're converting present-tense verbs to past-tense verbs.

What about irregular verbs, though? Yes, the English language's wild cards. These verbs do not follow the standard '-ed' rule and instead have their own distinct past-tense forms. Some spellings change completely, such as 'go' becoming 'went,' while others add a little something extra, such as 'eat' becoming 'ate.' Don't worry if it sounds a little confusing; we have plenty of examples to help you understand.

Finally, we'll go over how to construct negative and interrogative sentences in the simple past tense. Because, let's face it, there are times when you need to say things like, "I swear I didn't eat that last piece of cake!" or "Did you see what happened last night?" So, strap in and prepare to enter the wild and wonderful world of the simple past tense!

Assume you went to a party last night. Isn't that in the past? If you want to discuss it, use the Simple Past tense. "I danced all night at the party," for example.

Regular verbs in the Simple Past tense now typically end in "-ed." So, to say "walked" in the past, you say "walked." Isn't it simple?

There are, however, always exceptions. Irregular verbs have their own past tense forms, such as "go" becoming "went" or "eat" becoming "ate." It may appear confusing at first, but with practice, you'll get the hang of it!

Let's now look at how to construct negative and interrogative sentences in the Simple Past tense. We add "didn't" before the verb in negative sentences. "I didn't dance with anyone at the party," for example. In interrogative sentences, the subject and verb are switched. "Did you dance at the party?" for example.

Remember that the Simple Past tense is used for events that occurred in the past and are now finished. So, if you want to talk about your wild night at the party, use the Simple Past tense!

Here is a handy chart:

Subject	Positive	Negative	Question
I	I jumped.	I did not jump	Did I jump?
You	You worked	You didn't work	Did you work?
We	We danced	We didn't dance	Did we dance?
They	They listened	They did not listen	Did they listen?
He/She/It	He/She/It played	He/She/It played.	Did He/She/It play?

Simple, isn't it? Remember to practice the irregular verbs, and you will be fluent in no time!

Past Continuous Tense

Let's dive into the details of the past continuous/progressive tense now! This tense is used to describe past actions that were in progress. It's like watching a movie and seeing what happened at a specific point in time.

Assume you were watching a movie about a chef who was baking a cake. "The chef was mixing the batter when the oven suddenly exploded," you might say. The action of "mixing the batter" was in progress when the oven exploded in this case.

"Was/were" plus a present participle, such as "eating," "walking," or "playing," are common verbs used in the past continuous/progressive tense.

Let's look at how to construct negative and interrogative sentences in the past continuous/progressive tense. We add "not" after "was/were" to form a negative sentence. "The chef was not mixing the batter when the oven exploded," for example.

We switch the order of "was/were" and the subject to form an interrogative sentence. "Was the chef mixing the batter when the oven exploded?" for example.

Here's a handy chart to help you visualize this:

Subject	Positive	Negative	Question

I	I was walking.	I wasn't walking.	Was I walking?
You	You were eating.	You weren't eating.	Were you eating?
We	We were singing.	We weren't singing	Were we singing?
They	They were swimming.	They weren't swimming.	Were we swimming?
He/She/It	He/She/It was running.	He/She/It wasn't running.	Was He/She/It running?

Now, go forth and perfect your use of the past continuous/progressive tense!

Past Perfect Tense

Let's get started with the past perfect tense. Don't worry, it's not as frightening as it sounds. It's quite cool. The past perfect tense is used to describe an action that occurred prior to another action in the past. Consider it a step further back in time than the simple past tense.

Assume you're telling a story about how you lost your keys. "I had lost my keys before going to work," you could say. Because you lost your keys before going to work, you use the past perfect tense "had lost" to describe it.

Let's take a look at some common verbs used in the past perfect tense:

- had eaten.

- had slept.
- had studied.
- had watched.
- had finished.

Simply use "had" followed by the verb's past participle to form the past perfect tense. "I had breakfast before going to school," for example.

Let's now look at how to construct negative and interrogative sentences in the past perfect tense. Simply add "not" after "had" to make a negative sentence. "I hadn't finished my homework before class," for example.

Use the auxiliary verb "had" at the beginning of the sentence to form an interrogative sentence. "Had you eaten breakfast before leaving the house?" for example.

In a nutshell, that's the past perfect tense. More examples and different forms of the past perfect tense can be found in the chart below:

Subject	Positive	Negative	Question
I	I had eaten.	I hadn't eaten.	Had I eaten?
You	You had cried.	You hadn't cried.	Had you cried?

We	We had sung.	We hadn't sung.	Had we sung?
They	They had jumped.	They hadn't jumped	Had they jumped?
He/She/It	He/She/It had worked	He/She/It hadn't worked	Had he/she/it worked?

Past Perfect Continuous/Progressive Tense

If you're feeling brave, let's explore the world of the Past Perfect Continuous/Progressive Tense. Don't worry, it's not as difficult as it appears! Essentially, this tense is used to describe an action that began in the past and continued until another action occurred in the past.

Assume you were studying for an exam for four hours before your friend called. "I had been studying for 4 hours before my friend called," you can say. See how we used both the Past Perfect and the Continuous/Progressive tense to show that you were studying for a long time before your friend called?

The auxiliary verb "had" in the Past Perfect tense, the main verb "been" in the Present Participle form (-ing), and the main verb in the Past Participle form are required to form the Past Perfect Continuous/Progressive tense (-ed).

Here's an example of a conversation in the past perfect continuous/progressive tense:

Bob: "Hey, Jane, what were you doing before I arrived?"

Jane: "I had been cleaning the house all morning."

Bob: "Wow, that's a lot of work. Did you finish?"

Jane: "Yes, I had been cleaning for four hours straight. But then I took a break when you arrived."

Bob: "Ah, I see. Well, thanks for all your hard work!"

Jane uses the past perfect continuous/progressive tense in this dialogue to describe an action that began before a specific point in the past and was still ongoing at the time. She also describes what she did when Bob arrived in the past simple tense.

Subject	Auxiliary Verb	"Have been" Verb	Main Verb + "ing"	Object
I	Had	been	playing	All night
You	Had	been	jogging	For three hours
We	Had	been	cooking	dinner
They	Had	been	singing	songs
He/She/It	Had	been	working	hard

The auxiliary verb "had" is used in the past tense in this tense, followed by "been" and the main verb in the present participle form (ending in -ing). The phrase "have been" indicates that the action began in the past and continued until a specific point in the past. At the end of the sentence, the object can be added.

Key Takeaways

Simple Past Tense: It is used to describe an action that has already occurred in the past. Regular verbs are formed in the simple past tense by adding "-ed" to the base form of the verb, whereas irregular verbs have their own past tense forms.

The Past Continuous/Progressive Tense is used to describe an action that was taking place at a specific point in the past. It is formed by combining the past tense of the verb "to be" with the main verb's present participle (-ing form).

The Past Perfect Tense is used to describe an action that occurred prior to another action in the past. It is formed by combining the past participle of the verb "to have" with the main verb's past participle.

Past Perfect Continuous/Progressive Tense: It is used to define an ongoing process that was finished prior to an earlier past activity. It is created by combining the present participle (-ing form) of the primary verb with the past perfect tense of the verb "to be".

Make sure to reobserve before solving the test! I am sure you will do great!

Exercises

Fill in the blanks.

1) Last night, I _____ (eat) sushi with my friends.

2) While I _____ (watch) TV, the phone _____ (ring).

3) By the time I arrived, they _____ (finish) dinner.

4) They _____ (play) tennis for two hours before it started raining.

5) Yesterday, I _____ (walk) to the park with my dog.

6) While we _____ (wait) for the bus, it _____ (start) to snow.

7) She _____ (not study) for the exam, so she failed.

8) By the time we got to the movie theater, the movie _____ (already start).

9) I _____ (read) a book when the power went out.

10) They _____ (not see) the movie because they arrived too late.

11) By the time I got home, my parents _____ (cook) dinner.

12) He _____ (work) at the company for five years before he quit.

13) Last week, I _____ (visit) my grandparents in Florida.

14) While she _____ (listen) to music, she _____ (clean) her room.

15) By the time the guests arrived, we _____ (decorate) the house for the party.

Answer Key

1) "ate" (Simple Past tense)
2) "was watching" and "rang" (Past Continuous Tense)
3) "Had finished" (Past Perfect Tense)
4) "Had been playing" (Past Perfect Continuous/Progressive Tense)
5) "Walked" (Simple Past Tense)
6) "Were waiting, started" (Past Continuous/Progressive Tense)
7) "Did not study" (Simple Past Tense)
8) "had already started" (Past Perfect Tense)
9) "Was reading" (Past Continuous/Progressive Tense)
10) "Did not see" (Simple Past Tense)
11) "Had cooked" (Past Perfect Tense)
12) "Had been working" (Past Perfect Continuous/Progressive Tense)
13) "visited" (Simple Past Tense)
14) "Was listening, was cleaning" (Past Continuous/Progressive Tense)
15) "Had decorated" (Past Perfect Tense)

Congratulations, you've completed another chapter! You're one step closer to becoming a grammar genius, which is something to be proud of. Remember that consistency is the key to success, so keep practicing those past tenses until they become second nature. Don't be afraid to make mistakes; even the best of us make mistakes from time to time. Remember: if you don't succeed the first time, blame autocorrect and try again. You can do it!

Chapter 4: Future: A Journey to The Unknown

"The best way to predict your future is to create it."

- Abraham Lincoln

Welcome, time travelers! In this chapter, we'll venture into the unknown, delving into the world of future tense. "What is the future tense?" you may be wondering. It's not a crystal ball or a time machine, but it does allow us to make predictions and discuss events that have yet to occur. And, let's be honest, who doesn't enjoy a good prediction? So, buckle up and prepare to learn everything there is to know about the simple future tense, the future progressive/continuous tense, and the future perfect tense. You'll be able to predict the future like a pro by the end of this chapter!

Simple Future Tense

Are you prepared to forecast the future? So, buckle up and prepare your crystal ball, because we're about to enter the world of the Simple Future Tense!

The Simple Future Tense is used to describe an action that will occur in the future. It's like getting a glimpse into the future!

Let's start with an example dialogue:

"Hey, are you free tomorrow evening?" Maggie asks.

Joe: "Sure, I am. Why?"

Maggie: "I am hosting a party. Would you like to come?"

Joe: "Sure! What time does it begin?"

"It starts at 7 p.m.," Maggie says.

Joe: "Great! I'll be there."

Did you spot the future tense? Joe said, "I'll be there," (Short for "I will be there") indicating his intention to attend the party.

Making a sentence in the simple future tense is as simple as pie, or even easier if you're a terrible baker. Simply place the helping verb "will" before the base form of the verb. It's like making a promise to yourself or someone else about something that will happen in the future. "I'll dance like a chicken if I win the lottery," for example. It's really that simple! But be warned: if you break your promise, you may be forced to perform the chicken dance in public.

Positive ⌐↳ Subject + Will + base form of the verb

Negative ⌐↳ Subject + Will not (Won't) + base form of the verb

Question ⌐↳ Will + Subject + base form of the verb

So, there you have it, everyone! The future tense may appear to be an uncertain and mysterious place, but you can predict it with confidence using the simple future tense. Remember that the future is what you make of it, and you can shape it to your liking with the power of language. Whether you're discussing the weather for tomorrow, your plans for next week, or the next big adventure in your life, the simple future tense has you covered. So, my fellow language learners, go forth and conquer the future with the power of your words.

Future Progressive/Continuous Tense

Oh, the present progressive tense! A fancy way of saying that an action will continue in the future. So, what's the deal with this tense?

Future progressive/continuous tense definition and usage:

It's used to describe an ongoing action that will take place in the future. "I'll be studying for my exam tomorrow evening," for example. So, it's not just something that will happen in the future; it will happen all the time in the future.

Assume you're throwing a surprise birthday party for a friend. "I will be decorating the room while you keep her distracted," you could say. You could also say, "Take the left turn at the next intersection, and you'll be driving on the highway for the next few miles," if you're giving someone directions.

Let us now discuss how to construct negative and interrogative sentences. Simply add "not" after "will be" to form the negative. "I will not be working tomorrow," for example. Switch the subject and "will be" positions to form the interrogative. "Will you be studying for your exam next weekend?" for example.

To make things easier, here:

Positive ⌐→ Subject + Will be + verb +ing

Negative ⌐→ Subject + Will not (Won't) be + verb + ing

Question ⌐→ Will + Subject + be + verb + ing

Well, folks, that wraps up our journey into the future! We've learned all about the future progressive/continuous tense and how it can be used to describe ongoing future actions. Remember, it's all about adding that 'be' verb and the '-ing' ending to the main verb. So, whether you're going skydiving, binge-watching Netflix, or finally learning how to cook, describe your upcoming activities in the future progressive/continuous tense. The future may be unknown, but with this tense in your arsenal, you'll be ready for anything! Happy future-ing!

"Going to" Future Tense

The future tense "going to" is used to express actions that will occur in the future. It is frequently used to discuss plans, intentions, and predictions based on current evidence. It differs from the simple future tense in that it indicates that the speaker has already decided on the future action.

Example 1:

Amara: What do you have planned for the weekend?

Lisa: I am going to the airport.

Example 2:

Lisa: Why are you carrying a suitcase?

Alex: I'm going on vacation. I'll be in Hawaii.

To make a negative sentence in the future tense of "going to," insert "not" between "am/are/is" and "going to":

I'm not going to the party, for example.

To create an interrogative sentence in the future tense "going to," swap the subject and "am/are/is":

For instance, are you going to accompany me?

You might be thinking "This is just like "will". How am I supposed to differentiate them?" Here is a chart to help you:

Aspect	"Will"	"Going To"
Definition	Used for predictions or future certainty	Used for planned or pre-decided future events
Structure	Subject + will + verb (base form)	Subject + am/is/are + going to + verb (base form)
Usage	Used for sudden, spontaneous decisions	Used for premeditated decisions and plans
Example	"I'll help you with that."	"I'm going to help you with that."

Emphasis	Emphasizes the speaker's willingness.	Emphasizes the plan or intention.
Certainty	Less certain, more open to change.	More certain, less likely to change.
Time frame	Often used for distant future events.	Often used for near future events.
Connotation	Can be seen as more optimistic or positive.	Can be seen as more practical or realistic.
Predictive	Can be used to make predictions.	Rarely used to make predictions, instead used for pre-planned events.
Comics	"I will study hard tomorrow... but today... Zzzz."	"I am going to ace this exam; I have been studying all week."

I hope you find the comparison chart useful!

Future Perfect Tense

The future perfect tense is used to describe an action that will take place at a later date. This tense is formed by combining "will have + past participle" or "be going to have + past participle". It is important to note that the future perfect tense is used to describe an action that will be completed before a specific future time.

Here are some examples of how to use the future perfect tense:

- ✓ I'll have graduated from college by next year.
- ✓ The food will have been served by the time we arrive at the party.
- ✓ They will have been married for 25 months next month.

Negative: To form the negative in the future perfect tense, we use "will not have + past participle" or "be not going to have + past participle".

Example: By the end of this week, I will not have finished all my work.

Interrogative: To form the interrogative in the future perfect tense, we invert the subject and "will have" or "be going to have" and add the past participle.

Example: Will you have completed your project by tomorrow?

The following chart compares the future perfect tense to the other future tenses:

Tense	Structure	Example

Simple Future	Subject + will + base verb	I will travel to Europe next year.
"Going to" Future	Subject + be + going to + base verb	I am going to travel to Europe next year.
Future Perfect	Subject + will have + past participle or be going to have + past participle	I will have traveled to Europe by next year.

Congratulations, then! You have completed the Future Perfect Tense section! And if you've made it this far, you're already on your way to having perfect grammar in the future. Remember that with great power comes great responsibility, so use your newfound knowledge wisely and don't be afraid to show off your flawless future tense skills to all your friends. Who knows, maybe you'll become your social circle's future tense expert. Now, set out to conquer the future!

Key Takeaways

- ✓ The future tense is used to discuss events or actions that will take place in the future.
- ✓ To make predictions or discuss future events, use the simple future tense.
- ✓ The future progressive/continuous tense describes ongoing actions that will take place in the future.
- ✓ The future perfect tense is used to describe actions that will be completed at a later date.
- ✓ Both "will" and "going to" are used to discuss the future; however, "will" is more commonly used for predictions or

spontaneous decisions, whereas "going to" is used for plans or intentions.

✓ When it comes to negative sentences, "After "will" or "am/is/are going to," "not" is added.

✓ "The subject comes before "will" or "am/is/are going to" in question sentences.

Future Tenses Quiz

These Exercises Will Put Your Future Tense Knowledge to the Test! Prepare to Improve Your Language Skills and learn the skill of Future Talk.

Circle the correct form. If both are correct, circle both.

1. We _____ (will go / are going to go) to the beach this weekend.

2. By next year, I _____ (will have graduated / will graduate) from college.

3. She _____ (is going to have / will have) a baby next month.

4. They _____ (will finish / are finishing) their project tomorrow.

5. By the time he gets here, we _____ (will have prepared / will prepare) dinner.

6. I _____ (am meeting / will meet) my boss at 3 PM tomorrow.

7. By the end of the year, we _____ (will have saved / will save) enough money for our vacation.

8. She _____ (is going to start / will start) a new job next week.

9. They _____ (will have been married / will be married) for 10 years next month.

10. We _____ (are leaving / will leave) for the airport in an hour.

Answer Key

1. Answer: Both "will go" and "are going to go" are correct, as they both express future plans.
2. Answer: "will have graduated" is correct, as it expresses the completion of an action in the future that started before the future time reference.
3. Answer: Both "is going to have" and "will have" are correct, as they both express future events.
4. Answer: "will finish" is correct, as it expresses a future action that will happen after the time of speaking.
5. Answer: "will have prepared" is correct, as it expresses the completion of an action in the future that started before the future time reference.
6. Answer: Both "am meeting" and "will meet" are correct, as they both express future actions that are planned.
7. Answer: "will have saved" is correct, as it expresses the completion of an action in the future that started before the future time reference.
8. Answer: Both "is going to start" and "will start" are correct, as they both express future events.
9. Answer: "will have been married" is correct, as it expresses the completion of an action in the future that started before the future time reference.
10. Answer: Both "are leaving" and "will leave" are correct, as they both express future actions that are planned.

Well, well, well, we've made it to the end of our journey through the future tenses! I hope you're now feeling confident and ready to face the unknown that lies ahead. Remember, when it comes to predicting or talking about future events, you've got three powerful tools in your grammar toolbox: will, going to, and the future continuous. And when you need to describe actions that will be completed by a certain point in the future, don't forget about the trusty future perfect tense. So go forth and conquer the future with your newfound grammar skills, and remember: if you ever feel lost, just use 'will' and the power of positive thinking, and everything will be alright. Now, onto the next chapter!

Chapter 5: The Power of "If" Conditional Sentences and Passive Voice

"If you can't explain it simply, you don't understand it well enough."

- Albert Einstein

Welcome to the amazing world of "if" and passive voice! In this chapter, we'll look at two of the most effective tools in the English language. Conditional sentences enable us to consider hypothetical scenarios and what might happen if certain conditions are met. The passive voice, on the other hand, allows us to emphasize the subject of a sentence or add a polite tone to our speech.

But don't be put off by the technical jargon! With a little practice, you'll soon be crafting complex conditional sentences and effortlessly wielding the passive voice like a pro. So grab a cup of coffee (or tea, or hot chocolate, or whatever beverage you prefer), and prepare to unleash the full power of the English language!

Conditional Sentences

If you've ever wondered how to express hypothetical situations or discuss events that might or might not occur, you've come to the right place. We'll look at conditional sentences in this chapter, which are used to express conditions or possibilities. There are several types of conditional sentences, including the zero, first, second, third, and mixed conditionals.

A) Definition and usage of conditional sentences

Conditional sentences are sentences that express a condition and its effects. They usually begin with an "if" clause to introduce the condition, followed by a main clause that expresses the result.

❖ **Zero conditional tense, used for factual, general truths.**

The zero conditional tense is used to discuss always true facts or general truths. In both clauses, the present simple tense is used.

Forming zero conditional sentences is as follows: If + present simple tense, present simple tense.

Here are some examples of zero conditional sentences:

➢ If water is heated to 100 degrees Celsius, it boils!
➢ If you mix blue and red, you get purple!

❖ **First conditional tense, used for possible events in the future.**

The first conditional tense is used to discuss events that may occur in the future. It is formed using the present simple tense in the "if" clause and the future simple tense (will + base verb) in the main clause.

How to Create Your First Conditional Sentence:

If + present simple tense, will + base verb

First conditional sentence examples:

➤ If it rains tomorrow, I will stay at home.
➤ If I have time, I will call you later.

❖ **Second conditional tense, used for hypothetical or unusual present or future events.**

The second conditional tense is used to discuss hypothetical or improbable current or future events. The past simple tense is used in the "if" clause, and the conditional simple tense (would + base verb) is used in the main clause.

How to Create a Second Conditional Sentence:

If + past simple tense, would + base verb

Second conditional sentence examples:

➤ If I won the lottery, I would buy a house.
➤ If I were you, I would study harder.

❖ **Third conditional tense, used for hypothetical past events.**

The third conditional tense is used to discuss hypothetical past events that never occurred. The past perfect tense is used in the "if" clause, and the conditional perfect tense (would have + past participle) is used in the main clause.

Forming third conditional sentences:

If + past perfect tense, would have + past participle

Examples of third conditional sentences:

> ➢ If I had studied harder, I would have passed the exam.
> ➢ If I had known you were coming, I would have baked a cake.

❖ **Mixed conditionals are used in complex or mixed situations.**

Mixed conditionals are used in situations where the condition is in the past and the result is in the present or future, or vice versa. They can be created by combining different conditional sentence tenses.

Forming Mixed Conditional Sentences:

> ➢ If + past perfect tense, would + base verb (for the present or future result)
> ➢ If + past simple tense, would have + past participle (for the past result)

Examples of mixed conditional sentences:

> ➢ If I had studied harder, I would be working in a better job now.
> ➢ If I had gone to bed earlier last night, I wouldn't be so tired now.

This covers the basics of the different types of conditional sentences.

Passive Voice

Have you ever heard the phrase "mistakes were made" and wondered who made them? Perhaps you've seen a sentence that starts with "It was said" and wondered, "Who said it?" Welcome to the world of passive voice, where the subject of the sentence is frequently unknown or understated.

Passive voice can be confusing, but don't worry! We'll break it down for you in this chapter in a fun and understandable way. We'll look at what passive voice is, how it differs from active voice, and when it's appropriate to use it. By the end of this chapter, you'll be able to write clear and effective passive voice sentences. So, grab your thinking cap and let's dive into the world of passive voice!

Definition and usage of passive voice:

Simply put, passive voice is a sentence structure in which the subject of the sentence receives the action rather than performing it. In other words, the sentence's object becomes the subject. Instead of saying "The cat chased the mouse," we can say " Mouse was chased by the cat." This is an example of the passive voice.

Passive voice is frequently used to emphasize the object of the sentence rather than the subject, to make a sentence more polite, or to draw attention away from the person or thing performing the action.

How to form passive voice sentences:

A passive voice sentence requires a form of the auxiliary verb "to be" and the main verb's past participle. The structure is as follows:

subject + auxiliary verb (to be) + past participle + by + agent (optional)

For example, "The door was closed by the wind."

Passive voice sentence examples:

The passive voice can be used in a variety of contexts, ranging from academic writing to casual conversation. Here are a couple of examples:

- The cake was baked by my sister.
- The movie was watched by millions of people.
- That room was cleaned before.
- The car was repaired.
- The book was written by her.

The difference between active and passive voice is as follows:

Active voice, as compared to passive voice, is a sentence construction in which the subject performs the verb's action. In general, active voice is more direct and straightforward than passive voice.

For example, instead of saying "John wrote the book," we can say "John wrote the book." The second sentence is written in the active voice, which is clearer and more concise.

When should you use the passive voice?

While passive voice can be useful in some situations, active voice is generally preferred because it is clearer and far more straightforward. The passive voice, on the other hand, can be used in the following situations:

✓ When the emphasis is on the sentence's object rather than the subject.

✓ To avoid directly blaming or accusing someone.

✓ When the subject (the person or thing doing the action) is unknown or insignificant.

So now you know everything there is to know about passive voice!

Key Takeaways

- Conditional sentences and passive voice are two important grammar topics covered in this chapter.
- Conditional sentences are used to discuss hypothetical or factual situations, whereas passive voice is used to emphasize a sentence's object or to make a sentence more polite.
- Conditional sentences are classified into four types: zero, first, second, and third, as well as mixed conditionals, which combine elements of different types.
- General truths or scientific facts are expressed by zero conditional sentences.
- The first conditional sentence expresses a potential future condition and its outcome.
- The second conditional sentence expresses an unlikely or hypothetical present or future condition and its outcome.
- Third conditional sentences describe a possible past condition and its outcome.
- Mixed conditionals combine different types of elements to express more complex situations.
- The passive voice is formed by combining a form of the verb "to be" with the main verb's past participle.
- The passive voice can be used to emphasize a sentence's object or to make a sentence more polite.

The Importance of Understanding Conditionals and Passive Voice

Understanding conditional sentences and passive voice is critical for effective English communication. Conditional sentences are commonly used in everyday conversations and formal writing to express thoughts, wishes, and possibilities. Understanding the various conditional tenses allows you to communicate more precisely and effectively. Passive voice is also useful in English, particularly in formal writing, because it makes your sentences sound more objective and impersonal. Knowing when and how to use the passive voice can help you write clear, concise sentences that effectively convey your message.

Tips for Improving Your Conditional Sentences and Passive Voice Skills:

You can begin by practicing with various types of exercises and examples to improve your skills in using conditional sentences and passive voice. Reading and listening to English materials can also help you understand how conditional sentences and passive voice are used in everyday situations. It's also important to consider the context and purpose of the sentence before selecting the appropriate conditional tense or voice. Finally, don't be afraid to make and learn from mistakes, as this is an essential part of the learning process. You can understand conditional sentences and passive voice with practice and patience and become a confident and effective English communicator.

Exercises

1. If the car _____ (not fix) soon, it will break down on the highway.

2. The flowers _____ (water) every day if it doesn't rain.

3. If I _____ (win) the lottery, I would buy a house.

4. The letter _____ (send) by email yesterday.

5. If she _____ (study) harder, she would have passed the exam.

6. The concert _____ (postpone) due to bad weather.

7. If the food _____ (not cook) properly, it can make you sick.

8. The package _____ (deliver) tomorrow morning.

9. If they _____ (not arrive) on time, we will start without them.

Answer: do not arrive (First Conditional in Active Voice)

10. The book _____ (read) by millions of people around the world.

Answer: has been read (Present Perfect Passive Voice)

Answer Key

1. Answer: is not fixed (First Conditional in Passive Voice)
2. Answer: need to be watered (Simple Present Passive Voice)
3. Answer: won (Second Conditional in Active Voice)
4. Answer: was sent (Simple Past Passive Voice)
5. Answer: had studied (Third Conditional in Active Voice)
6. Answer: was postponed (Simple Past Passive Voice)
7. Answer: is not cooked (First Conditional in Passive Voice)
8. Answer: will be delivered (Simple Future Passive Voice)
9. Answer: do not arrive (First Conditional in Active Voice)
10. Answer: has been read (Present Perfect Passive Voice)

Congratulations, my friend! You passed the passive voice, and conditional sentence quiz! You've grasped verb tenses and sentence structures. You've probably spent more time than most people do in a lifetime thinking about grammar. But don't worry! You can now use your newly acquired language skills to impress your friends, family, and pets. Who knows, maybe you'll start correcting people's grammar in public! Just keep in mind that with great grammar comes great responsibility. Don't be a grammar snob when using it. Continue to practice and stay tuned for more language adventures!

Chapter 6: Modal Verbs: The Power of Possibility

"Modal verbs allow us to talk about the world as we imagine it could be, should be, or might be."

- Ronald Carter

Welcome to Chapter 6, where we'll delve into the bizarre realm of modal verbs! Let me tell you why this chapter is going to be so much fun before you start yawning and scrolling through your social media feeds. Modal verbs, you see, are like the spice rack of English grammar; they offer flavor, diversity, and a little zing to your phrases. Your English would be as dull as a dish of porridge without them. This chapter is for those who wish to improve their language skills and amaze their peers.

We'll be delving deep into the power of possibility in this chapter - and no, I'm not talking about the chance of finding a unicorn in your backyard (although that would be pretty cool). I'm referring to the ability to express yourself in new and fascinating ways by employing modal verbs. Everything from ability and possibility to obligation and necessity will be discussed. We'll even look into the future and make some predictions - no, I don't have a crystal ball, but I do have some pretty cool modal verbs up my sleeve.

I know what you're thinking: "What are modal verbs? Sounds boring." But believe me, we're going to have a great time. We'll make studying modal verbs as entertaining as watching a comedy movie by combining humor, real-life examples, and interactive exercises (okay, maybe not that fun, but close). By the end of this chapter, you'll be a modal verb expert, confidently employing these little powerhouses. Now grab some popcorn and prepare to enter the wild and wacky world of modal verbs!

Understanding Modal Verbs

Modal verbs are English verbs that express the speaker's attitude toward the activity or state of being mentioned in the sentence. Because these verbs lack a distinct tense, they do not alter form to signify past, present, or future time.

These are a few instances of modal verbs:

- Can: used to show ability, possibility, or permission
- Could: used to show ability, possibility, or past ability
- Shall: used to make suggestions or offer assistance
- Should: used to give advice or make suggestions
- Will: used to show future certainty or willingness
- Would: used to show past habits, willingness, or hypothetical situations
- May: used to show possibility or permission
- Might: used to show possibility or past possibility
- Must: used to show necessity or obligation

It is vital to notice that each modal verb has its own distinct meaning and application and employing them effectively will help you enhance your English language skills significantly. In the following sections, we will go over each modal verb in greater depth and provide examples of how to utilize them in various contexts.

Expressing Ability and Possibility

Are you tired of repeating yourself every time someone asks whether you can do something? Goodbye, dull responses, and hello, the power of modal verbs! You can communicate your capacity and capability in a fun and engaging way by using can, could, may, and might.

When asked if you can speak Spanish, for example, instead of simply replying "yes," you may say "I can speak Spanish like a native!" If someone asks you to pass the salt, you can say, "I could pass you the salt blindfolded!"

- ✓ **Can:** This modal verb indicates that someone is capable of doing something. "I speak English fluently," for example.

- ✓ **Could:** Could, like can, is used to demonstrate capacity, but it can also be used to demonstrate past ability. "When I was younger, I could run a mile in under 5 minutes," for example.

- ✓ **May:** This modal verb expresses possibilities. For example, "It may rain tomorrow, so bring an umbrella."

- ✓ **Might:** Similar to may, might is used to indicate possibilities. Nonetheless, it is more commonly employed to express uncertainty than may. "I might go to the beach this weekend if the weather is pleasant," for example.

We've made a simple chart to help you recall the rules for using these modal verbs:

Modal Verb	Function	Example
Can	Ability	I can drive a car.
Could	Ability (past), Polite Request	I could drive a car when I was younger.
May	Possibility	It may rain today.
Might	Possibility (less certain than "may")	I might go to the party tomorrow.

We've also included some activities to help you practice correctly using these modal verbs. As an example:

✓ "I _____ play the piano when I was younger," finish the phrase.
  o The answer is "could."

✓ "I _____ go to the movies tonight if I finish my homework."
  o The answer is "may."

So, you now understand the fundamentals of employing can, could, may, and might to communicate ability and probability. Keep practicing, and you'll soon be a modal verb expert!

Expressing Obligation and Necessity

Following that are the modal verbs, which indicate duty and necessity. These are musts and should. Let's look more closely:

Must: This modal verb indicates that something is required or necessary. "I need to finish my homework before I can watch TV," for example.

Should: This modal verb is used to indicate that something is advisable but not required. "You should eat breakfast every day for optimal health," for example.

Here's a visual reminder of how to utilize these modal verbs:

Modal Verb	Function	Example
Must	Necessity	I must go to bed early tonight.
Should	Advice	You should drink plenty of water every day.

To practice using these modal verbs correctly, try completing the following sentence:

✓ "I _____ wear a helmet while riding my bike for safety."
  ○ Answer: "must"

Expressing Prediction and Future Possibility

Will and would are modal verbs that communicate prediction and future potential. Here's what you should know:

Will: This modal verb indicates that something is assured to happen in the future. "I will graduate from college next year," for example. (I know you remember "Will" from previous chapters!)

Would: This modal verb is used to describe a hypothetical or future possibility. "If I won the lotto, I would purchase a house," for example.

For more information, consult the following chart:

Modal verb	Function	Example
Will	Prediction	It will rain tomorrow.
Would	Hypothetical situations	If I had more time, I would travel more often.

Here's a practice activity to help you use will and would:

✓ "If I had more money, I _____ buy a new car," complete the phrase.
  ○ "Would" is the correct response.

Expressing Advice and Probability

Finally, modal verbs are used to indicate advice and possibility. These are the words may, might, and should. Let's get started:

May and Might: As previously stated, these modal verbs express possibilities. They can, however, be used to express probability or likelihood. "It might rain later, so I'll bring an umbrella," for example.

Should: This modal verb has been used before, but this time it is employed to indicate advice or a proposal. "You should try the sushi at that place; it's fantastic!" for example. (We have already discussed it above!)

Have a look at this chart to help you remember how to use these modal verbs:

Modal Verb	Function	Example
May/Might	Probability	I might go to the gym later if I have time.
Should	Advice	You should study for your exams if you want to do well.

Here's an exercise to help you practice using may, might, and should:

Choose the correct modal verb to complete the sentence:

✓ "It _____ snow tomorrow, so we should bring warm coats."
  ○ Answer: "might"

Common Mistakes and How to Avoid Them

It is normal for students to make mistakes when learning to use modal verbs. In this section, we'll go over some of the most prevalent blunders and offer advice and tactics for preventing them.

It is normal for students to make mistakes when learning to use modal verbs. In this section, we'll go over some of the most prevalent blunders and offer advice and tactics for preventing them.

One typical error is to mix up the words "can" with "could" when expressing ability. "Can" refers to current ability, whereas "could" refers to prior ability or ability in a hypothetical situation. For example, "I can speak French" suggests that you can speak French now, whereas "I could speak French when I was younger" means that you could speak French in the past. To illustrate hypothetical skill, a statement like "I could speak French fluently" is used.

Another typical error is to indicate necessity with "should" rather than "must." "Should" denotes a proposal or recommendation, but "must" denotes a severe requirement. For example, "You should study for the exam" suggests that studying is a good idea, whereas "You must study for the exam" means that studying is extremely vital.

To avoid these and other errors, practice using modal verbs in various circumstances and pay attention to the specific rules for each modal verb. You will be able to employ modal verbs more confidently and effectively in your communication as you get more familiar with their usage and meaning.

Key Takeaways

❖ Modal verbs are auxiliary verbs that communicate many different meanings in a sentence.

❖ In English, the most common modal verbs are can, could, may, might, must, must, should, will, and would.

❖ Ability, possibility, necessity, prediction, advice, and likelihood are all expressed using modal verbs.

❖ "Can" refers to present capacity, whereas "could" refers to past or hypothetical ability.

❖ "Should" denotes a proposal or recommendation, but "must" denotes a severe requirement.

❖ To avoid common errors, it is critical to pay attention to the unique rules for each modal verb.

❖ To improve your comprehension and usage of modal verbs, practice using them in diverse circumstances.

Review and Practice

Now that you've learned about modal verbs and their various applications, it's time to put what you've learned into practice. The tasks that follow will help you strengthen your understanding of modal verbs and enhance your ability to use them effectively.

Exercise 1: Complete the sentences with the correct modal verb.

1. I _____ swim when I was younger.
2. You _____ try the new restaurant in town.
3. We _____ have to leave early to catch the train.
4. _____ you please pass me the salt?
5. She _____ have forgotten about the meeting.

Exercise 2: Use a modal verb to communicate a different meaning in the following sentences.

1. I have to go to the dentist tomorrow.
2. You should study more if you want to pass the exam.
3. He will arrive at the airport at 7 pm.
4. She must have left her phone at home.
5. They are going to have a party tonight.

Exercise 3: Choose the correct modal verb to complete the sentences.

1. I _____ finish this report by tomorrow.
   a) must
   b) may
   c) could

2. _____ you please turn off the lights before you leave?
   a) may
   b) should
   c) will

3. I _____ speak Spanish fluently when I was living in Spain.
   a) could
   b) would
   c) can

4. She _____ be at work by 9 am.
   a) must
   b) could
   c) will

5. You _____ to try the new coffee shop on Main Street.
   a) may
   b) should
   c) would

Answer Key:

Exercise 1: 1. could 2. should 3. will 4. Could 5. may

Exercise 2: 1. I might have to go to the dentist tomorrow. 2. If you study more, you can pass the exam. 3. He may arrive at the airport at 7 pm. 4. She could have left her phone at home. 5. They might have a party tonight.

Exercise 3: 1. must 2. should 3. could 4. must 5. Should

Chapter 7: The Art of Expression: Gerunds and Infinitives

"The more languages you know, the more you are human."

- Tomáš Garrigue Masaryk

Welcome to the land of gerunds and infinitives, the two most interesting verb forms in English (yes, we said it). We understand that the very idea of grammar makes some people want to flee but trust us when we say that gerunds and infinitives are a piece of cake.

We'll take you on a crazy ride through the world of gerunds and infinitives in this chapter, showing you how to use them like a pro and impressing all your English-speaking friends. Who knows, maybe you'll start dreaming about them at night (we won't judge).

So, get ready to channel your inner grammar nerd and explore the fascinating world of gerunds and infinitives. You'll be using them like a boss (or a queen, we don't discriminate) by the conclusion of this chapter. Let's get started!

Understanding Gerunds and Infinitives

Gerunds and infinitives, oh my! What exactly are they, you ask? Let me explain in the simplest terms possible. A gerund is a verb that has been transformed into a noun by adding -ing at the end. Consider it the verb's superhero outfit, ready to save the day as a noun. Meanwhile, infinitives are the purest form of a verb, uncontaminated by any other word. It's like a tiny baby verb, full of potential and eager to develop.

Let's talk about their functions in a sentence now that you know what they are. Gerunds function similarly to nouns in that they can be the subject, direct object, or object of a preposition in a sentence. Infinitives, on the other hand, can function as nouns, adjectives, or adverbs depending on their context.

Gerunds as Subjects and Objects

Gerunds can be used as more than just nouns or adverbs. They can also be used in sentences as subjects or objects. This may appear complicated, but don't worry, we'll make it simple and enjoyable!

Gerunds as Subjects

We simply use the -ing form of a verb at the beginning of a sentence to use gerunds as subjects. As an example:

- Skiing is my favorite hobby.
- Singing loudly is not appropriate in a library.
- Running for exercise is good for your health.

As you can see, the gerund is used as the subject at the beginning of each sentence.

Gerunds as Objects

Gerunds can also function as objects in sentences. We simply use the -ing form of a verb after a verb or preposition to use gerunds as objects. As an example:

- I enjoy skiing on the weekends.
- He suggested singing a song together.
- She is good at running long distances.

The gerund is used as the object after a verb or preposition in each of these examples.

Gerunds can be difficult to use as subjects and objects, but with practice, you'll get the hang of it. Here is a chart with the rules for using gerunds as subjects and objects to assist you:

Gerunds as Subjects	Gerunds as Objects
Use -ing form of verb at beginning of sentence	Use -ing form of verb after a verb or preposition
Example: Dancing makes me happy.	Example: He is afraid of swimming.

Now it's your turn to practice using gerunds as subjects and objects!

Gerunds and Infinitives with Verbs

Gerunds and infinitives can also be combined with verbs to form a variety of sentences. They can, for example, be used as the object of a verb or as the subject of a sentence.

Let's look at some examples to better understand how to use gerunds and infinitives with verbs:

- She enjoys cooking. (Gerund as the object of the verb "enjoys")
- I want to learn how to dance. (Infinitive as the object of the verb "want")
- Swimming is good exercise. (Gerund as the subject of the sentence)

Here are some guidelines to follow when using gerunds and infinitives with verbs:

- ✓ After verbs like enjoy, avoid, and practice, use a gerund.
- ✓ When discussing a general activity, use a gerund as the subject of a sentence.
- ✓ When discussing a specific activity, use an infinitive as the subject of a sentence.
- ✓ After certain verbs, such as want, plan, and decide, use an infinitive.

Recall that gerunds and infinitives can be combined with modal verbs like should, would, and could to convey varying degrees of necessity or potential.

Don't be scared to use gerunds and infinitives with verbs to spice up your writing and speaking.

Gerunds and Infinitives with Adjectives and Adverbs

When combined with adjectives and adverbs, gerunds and infinitives can add meaning and depth to your statements. In this section, we'll look at how to do it effectively.

Gerunds and infinitives can describe feelings or attitudes when combined with adjectives. "I was delighted to see you," for example, utilizes the verb "to see" to express happiness.

When combined with adverbs, gerunds and infinitives can explain how something is done. "She walked gently, taking her time," for example, utilizes the gerund "taking" to indicate how she walked.

- ✓ **Adjective:** "I am excited to go on vacation"

✓ **Adverb:** "He spoke quickly, trying to finish his presentation"

Note that using gerunds and infinitives with adjectives and adverbs adds diversity and depth to your writing. So, why not give it a shot?

Expressing Purpose with Gerunds and Infinitives

In a sentence, gerunds and infinitives can also be employed to show purpose. This is a sophisticated way of expressing that they can demonstrate the motivation or intent behind an action. Here's how you can put them to use:

Using Gerunds to Express Purpose

When using gerunds to show intention, you can add "-ing" to a verb to make it a noun. Here are a couple of such examples:

- ✓ I went running to improve my health.
- ✓ She started learning French for her upcoming trip to Paris.
- ✓ They are practicing singing to perform at the talent show.

Use these rules when using gerunds to indicate purpose:

- Begin with a verb and add "-ing" to create a gerund.
- Use the gerund as the sentence's subject or object.
- To demonstrate the aim or intention, use words like "to" or "for."

Using Infinitives to Express Purpose

Infinitives are verbs that are generally followed by the word "to." They can also be used to convey intent in a sentence. Here are a couple of such examples:

- ✓ He took a cooking class to impress his girlfriend.
- ✓ She needs to study hard to get into a good college.
- ✓ They plan to travel the world to experience different cultures.

Use these rules when using infinitives to communicate purpose:

- To make an infinitive, begin with "to" and then a verb.
- Use the infinitive as the sentence's subject or object.
- To demonstrate the aim or intention, use words like "to" or "for."

That's all there is to it! Employing gerunds and infinitives to indicate purpose can improve the readability of your sentences and demonstrate your meaning behind an action. Just remember to stick to the rules, and you'll be expressing your intent like a pro in no time.

Common Mistakes and How to Avoid Them

Let's face it, folks. Gerunds and infinitives may be difficult little suckers. So don't be alarmed! By avoiding these typical errors, you can quickly become a gerund and infinitive expert.

1. It's all too simple to mix up gerunds and present participles. They appear to be almost similar, yet they have different roles in a phrase. Remember that gerunds function as nouns, whereas present participles function as adjectives or as components of verb tenses.

2. Overuse of the infinitive form: Infinitives are wonderful, but they are not the answer to every grammatical difficulty. Use them only when a gerund or another grammatical form would suffice.

3. Employing the incorrect preposition: When used with gerunds or infinitives, some verbs require certain prepositions. "I'm good at singing," for example, is correct, but "I'm good in singing" is incorrect.

4. Misplacing the infinitive marker "to": This is a classic. Just remember that "to" always comes before the verb's infinitive form.

5. Ignoring that gerunds and infinitives are not interchangeable: While they can both act as nouns, they have different uses in a phrase. Check that you're using the proper form for the situation.

Go forth and conquer those gerunds and infinitives now that you know what to look out for!

Key Takeaways

- Gerunds and infinitives are verb forms that can be utilized in sentences as nouns or adverbs.
- Gerunds finish in -ing, whereas infinitives begin with the verb "to."
- Gerunds and infinitives can be employed in sentences as subjects, objects, or complements.
- Gerunds and infinitives can be used with verbs, adjectives, and adverbs to convey a variety of meanings.
- Learners should pay attention to the verbs and prepositions used with gerunds and infinitives to prevent common errors.

-

Exercises and Activities

1. Identify whether the underlined verb is a gerund or infinitive:

a) I love singing in the shower.

b) I need to go to the grocery store to buy some milk.

c) Swimming is my favorite form of exercise.

d) My goal is to learn Spanish.

2. Choose the correct form (gerund or infinitive) to complete the sentence:

a) She offered _____ me a ride home. (drive, driving)

b) I hope _____ the chance to visit Japan someday. (to have, having)

c) The teacher encouraged _____ hard for the exam. (study, studying)

d) My parents want _____ me to get a good education. (for, to)

3. Rewrite the sentence using the given gerund or infinitive:

a) I like to watch a movie. (gerund: watching)

b) She likes to eat sushi. (gerund: eating)

c) He forgot taking his keys. (infinitive: to take)

d) They need more studying. (infinitive: to study)

4. Fill in the blanks with the correct gerund or infinitive:

a) I enjoy _____ (read) books in my free time.

b) He decided _____ (quit) his job and travel the world.

c) They agreed _____ (meet) at the restaurant at 7 pm.

d) She suggested _____ (take) the train instead of driving.

Answer Key:

1- a) gerund, b) infinitive, c) gerund, d) infinitive

2- a) driving, b) to have, c) studying, d) for

3- a) I like watching a movie. b) She likes eating sushi. c) He forgot to take his keys. d) They need to study more.

4- a) reading, b) to quit, c) to meet, d) taking

Congratulations! You've mastered the use of gerunds and infinitives in English. With this information, you may now confidently and precisely convey your ideas.

Note that utilizing gerunds and infinitives might help you sound more natural while speaking and writing. Continue to practice and incorporate these verb forms into your language.

Always keep in mind the different ways gerunds and infinitives can be used, such as as subjects, objects, and to express purpose, and how they can be used with different parts of speech.

And of course, don't forget to avoid common mistakes and use proper punctuation and capitalization to enhance the clarity of your writing.

So go forth and continue to learn, grow, and express yourself with confidence and precision. Good luck!

Chapter 8: Punctuation and Capitalization for Clarity

"I believe that the comma is one of the most important inventions in the history of punctuation."

- Mary Norris

Hello, and welcome to the bizarre world of punctuation and capitalization! Others may argue that these little marks and capital letters are insignificant in the great scheme of things. Yet, if you've ever been misinterpreted or puzzled by a statement due to improper punctuation or wrong capitalization, you understand how crucial these little guys can be. In this chapter, we'll look at the fundamentals of punctuation and capitalization and how they may make or break clear and successful communication. Prepare to master these little but powerful tools and take your English to the next level!

Basic Punctuation Marks

Punctuation marks, oh my. Those little squiggles and dots that can make or break a sentence. We'll go through the fundamentals of punctuation marks in this chapter, including periods, commas, semicolons, colons, apostrophes, quote marks, hyphens, and dashes.

Let us begin with ***periods***. You know, those little dots that indicate the end of a phrase. It's easy, but it's critical. Without periods, sentences would just go on and on... you get the picture.

Then there are **commas.** That dreadful comma. It's one of the most misused punctuation symbols. But don't worry, we'll go over some basic guidelines to help you utilize commas effectively.

The **semicolon** comes next. It's as if a comma and a period had a child. It's used to divide two related clauses that may stand on their own as sentences but should be linked together.

Colons and **dashes** may appear scary, but they are really rather easy to use. A colon introduces a list or emphasizes something, whereas a dash creates a pause or indicates an abrupt shift in thought.

Let's speak about **apostrophes** now. They are employed in contractions and possessives. It's a little detail, but appropriately employing apostrophes may make a significant impact on how your work is interpreted.

To denote direct speaking, **quotation marks** are employed, and **hyphens** are used to connect words that work together to express something.

Phew! It was a lot, but don't be concerned. We'll go through a lot of examples and activities to help you understand each punctuation mark. Well, let's get this party started!

A period (.) indicates the conclusion of a sentence:

- o   For instance, she went to the supermarket to get some food.

A comma (,) is used to divide items in a list, two clauses in a complex sentence, or phrases inside a sentence:

- o   Example 1 (list): He went to the store and bought apples, bananas, and oranges.

- o Example 2 (complex sentence): She studied diligently for the exam, yet she still fared poorly.
- o Example 3 (phrases): After finishing her homework, she went to bed.

Semicolon (;) - used to separate two unrelated independent clauses:

- o For example, she enjoys reading and spends much of her leisure time in the library.

Colon (:) - used to begin a list, quote, or explanation:

- o Example 1 (list): She needs the following items for her trip: a suitcase, a passport, and a camera.
- o Example 2 (quotation): The teacher said: "You need to submit your paper by next Friday."
- o Example 3 (explanation): He had only one goal: to become the best basketball player in the world.

Apostrophe (') - used to show possession or to indicate the omission of letters in a word:

- o Example 1 (possession): That is Mary's bike.
- o Example 2 (omission): It's raining outside (contraction of "it is").

Quotation marks (") - used to enclose direct speech or a quotation:

- o Example: She said, "I'll meet you at the park at 2 pm."

Hyphen (-) - used to connect two or more words that act as a single idea or to indicate a word break at the end of a line:

- o Example 1 (single idea): She is a well-known actress.

○ Example 2 (word break): I have a long-term project due next month.

Dash (--) - used to indicate a sudden change in thought or to add emphasis:

○ Example 1 (change in thought): She has two sisters--no, three.
○ Example 2 (emphasis): I have never--never--seen such a beautiful sunset.

As always, here's a chart to make things easier!

Punctuation Mark	Function	Example
Period	Indicates the end of a sentence	She loves playing video games.
Comma	Separates items in a list, separates clauses in a sentence, or separates parts of a sentence for clarity	I bought apples, bananas, and oranges at the store. She walked to the store, but it was closed. The cat, which was black and white, was sleeping.
Semicolon	Separates two related independent clauses	She loves to read; her favorite book is "Lord of The Rings."
Colon	Introduces a list, explanation, or quotation	She needed three things: bread, milk, and eggs. He had one problem: he couldn't find his keys. He

		quoted his favorite line from the movie: "Here's looking at you, kid."
Apostrophe	Indicates possession or contraction	The dog's tail wagged. She didn't want to go to the store.
Quotation Marks	Indicate direct speech or a quote	She said, "I'll be there soon." He quoted Shakespeare's famous line, "To be or not to be, that is the question."
Hyphen	Joins words together to create a compound word or to clarify meaning	She had a three-year-old son. The green-eyed monster was jealous.
Dash	Used to emphasize or separate a clause in a sentence	He wanted to go to the store--but it was closed. The book--which was on the shelf--fell to the ground.

Capitalization Guidelines

Are you annoyed by people always criticizing your spelling and grammar on the internet? It's about time they got a taste of their own medicine! In this chapter, we'll look at punctuation and capitalization, two aspects of writing that may make or break you. We'll go over everything from commas to colons and even toss in a few semicolons for good measure. Don't worry, we'll make it simple, so you don't have to hurry to your English teacher for help (unless you want to show off your newfound skills, of course). So, strap in and prepare to punctuate like a pro!

Proper Nouns

Proper nouns are particular names for individuals, places, objects, and concepts. Proper nouns should always be capitalized.

Now, let's get started and make sure we're all on the same page with capitalization. We'll start with the fundamentals:

- In a sentence, capitalize the initial letter of the first word.
- Proper nouns, which are the names of distinct individuals, places, and things, should be capitalized (e.g., John, London, Coca-Cola).
- Except for articles, prepositions, and conjunctions, capitalize the initial letter of every word in a title (e.g., The Catcher in the Rye).
- If the quotation is a whole phrase, capitalize the initial letter of the first word, but not if it is a fragment.

Now, let's look at some frequent mistakes to avoid:

- Common nouns should not be capitalized unless they are part of a title or used as a proper noun.
- Do not capitalize the initial letter of each word in a sentence or title (unless it is title case).
- Articles, prepositions, and conjunctions should not be capitalized in titles (unless they are the initial word).

I hope that clarifies things for you! And just in case it doesn't, I'll include a helpful chart with all the capitalization requirements.

Type of Word	Example	Rule
Proper Nouns	Los Angeles, Jack, Sprite	Capitalize the first letter of a proper noun
Titles	Dr. Oz, President Obama	Capitalize the first letter of each word in a title, except for prepositions, conjunctions, and articles
First Letter of a Sentence	The quick brown fox jumps over the lazy dog.	Capitalize the first letter of the first word in a sentence

Punctuation for Clarity

I want to thank all the punctuation marks out there before we continue with this section since they work so hard to help our written words make sense. We are all aware that a comma or semicolon put incorrectly can result in some humorous (and frequently embarrassing) misunderstandings. But worry not, dear reader, for in this part, we will delve into the lovely realm of punctuation and explore how it may be used to clarify meaning.

To begin with, let's take a closer look at how punctuation marks can change the meaning of a sentence. For instance, consider the difference between "Let's eat, Grandma!" and "Let's eat Grandma!"

The placement of that comma completely alters the meaning of the sentence, doesn't it? Poor Grandma would be terrified if we forgot to use that all-important comma. To begin with, let's take a deeper look at how punctuation marks can modify the meaning of a statement. Take the difference between "Let's eat, Grandma!" and "Let's eat Grandma!" For instance, it's obvious how the comma's placement affects the sentence's meaning. Poor Grandma would be scared if we neglected to utilize that all-important comma. After all, nobody wants to eat their grandma, right?

But don't lose sight of the greater picture. The primary goal of punctuation is to make our writing clearer and more intelligible. We may eliminate ambiguity and assure the accuracy of our communication by carefully employing punctuation marks. Therefore, let us welcome our punctuation friends and learn how to use them to our benefit!

Common Punctuation Mistakes and How to Avoid Them

Error #1: Using too many commas. Some people place a comma after every word in a phrase, which can cause confusion and break the flow of the text.

Solution: Only use commas where necessary to clarify meaning or to divide items in a list.

Error #2: Incorrect use of apostrophes. Many individuals are unsure when to use apostrophes to show possession or contraction.

Solution: Note that apostrophes are only used to signify possession or contraction, not plurals. "The cat's tail," for example, indicates that the tail belongs to the cat, but "The cats are playing" is the plural form and does not require an apostrophe.

Error #3: Forgetting to employ quote marks correctly. Many individuals are confused about where to put quote marks, whether indicating direct speech or a quotation from another source.

Solution: Use single or double quotation marks at the beginning and conclusion of the cited item, depending on the context.

Error #4: Incorrect use of semicolons and colons. Semicolons and colons may be highly beneficial in clarifying the link between distinct sections of a phrase, but they can also cause confusion if used wrongly.

Solution: Separate two distinct sentences that are closely connected with semicolons, then insert a list or explanation using colons.

Error #5: Ignoring the significance of punctuation entirely. Some people just ignore punctuation, which can make their writing difficult to read and understand.

Solution: Learn the fundamental laws of punctuation and practice applying them appropriately. Keep in mind that proper punctuation may substantially increase the clarity and effectiveness of your work.

Key Takeaways

- Punctuation markers such as periods, commas, and semicolons are vital in written communication for communicating meaning.
- Capitalization rules assist readers in differentiating between proper nouns, titles, and normal terms.
- Punctuation and capitalization can help to improve the clarity and effectiveness of your writing.
- Commas, which serve to divide clauses and phrases, are very useful for clarifying the meaning of a sentence.

- Typical punctuation errors include using too many or too few commas, putting them in the wrong place, and capitalizing incorrectly.
- To avoid punctuation issues, review your work thoroughly and utilize a style guide as a reference.
- To enhance your communication abilities, practice utilizing proper punctuation and capitalization in your writing.

Remember that understanding punctuation and capitalization will help you guarantee that your written communication is clear, effective, and simple to grasp. Good luck with your writing!

Exercises and Activities

Identify the punctuation errors in the following sentences:

a. Sarah's favorite colors are blue pink and purple.

b. The dog ran around the yard, barked at the mailman and chased the ball.

c. After dinner we went for a walk then we watched a movie.

Rewrite the following sentences with correct capitalization:

a. john lives in new york city and works as a lawyer.

b. my favorite food is pizza, and my favorite drink is cola.

c. the book of genesis is the first book in the old testament.

Add the correct punctuation to the following sentences:

a. i went to the store bought some apples and bananas and came home.

b. the party starts at 8 pm make sure to bring a gift.

c. he said i'll be there at 7 o'clock.

Rewrite the following sentences for clarity by adding or changing punctuation marks:

a. The panda eats shoots and leaves.

b. Let's eat Grandma!

c. She took a photograph of her parents, the president and the vice president.

Correct the capitalization errors in the following titles:

a. the lord of the rings: the fellowship of the ring

b. gone with the wind

c. harry potter and the sorcerer's stone

Answer Key

1a. Sarah's favorite colors are blue, pink, and purple.

1b. The dog ran around the yard, barked at the mailman, and chased the ball.

1c. After dinner, we went for a walk, then we watched a movie.

2a. John lives in New York City and works as a lawyer.

2b. My favorite food is pizza, and my favorite drink is cola.

2c. The Book of Genesis is the first book in the Old Testament.

3a. I went to the store, bought some apples and bananas, and came home.

3b. The party starts at 8 pm – make sure to bring a gift.

3c. He said, "I'll be there at 7 o'clock."

4a. The panda eats shoots, and leaves.

4b. Let's eat, Grandma!

4c. She took a photograph of her parents, the President, and the Vice President.

5a. The Lord of the Rings: The Fellowship of the Ring

5b. Gone with the Wind

5c. Harry Potter and the Sorcerer's Stone

Chapter 9: Writing and Speaking in English

"The pen is the tongue of the mind."

\- Horace

Welcome to the exciting world of English writing and speaking! This chapter is all about tickling your funny bone while also changing you into a communication expert. What's the use of learning a language if you can't make people laugh while doing it?

We'll dig deep into the importance of writing and speaking in English in this chapter because, let's face it, you don't want your newly acquired grammar abilities to go to waste. You've been honing your English skills, and it is finally time to show them off!

Our goal is to help you put together your ever-growing library of vocabulary and grammar rules and convert them into spectacular, humorous, and fascinating sentences that will make native speakers laugh and respect your language skills.

Now grab your favorite pen, put on your thinking cap, and prepare for a wild ride as we explore the wonderfully bizarre world of writing and speaking in English!

Section 1: Creating Complete Sentences

1.1   Understanding sentence structure: subject, verb, and object.

The classic trio of subject, verb, and object. Consider them the English language's Three Musketeers: inseparable and always ready for action! You've met them before, so let's just catch up, shall we?

In a sentence, the subject is the doer, the verb is the action, and the object is the receiver of the action. Like a well-choreographed dance routine, they must work together in harmony.

- Subject - Verb - Object
- The cat (subject) chased (verb) the mouse (object).

Now, behold the magic of a visual representation!

- [Subject] -> [Verb] -> [Object]
- [The cat] -> [chased] -> [the mouse]

1.2   Independent and Dependent Clauses

This is when things start to get interesting. There are two kinds of clauses in sentence structure: independent and dependent.

Independent clauses can function as whole sentences on their own (just like a proud, independent individual). They contain a subject and a verb and express an entire thought.

Dependent clauses, on the other hand, are like clingy partners. They can't stand on their own because they don't express an entire notion. They always require an independent clause to fall back on.

- The cat chased the mouse, which was an independent clause.
- Because it was hungry, dependent clause.

1.3   Combining Clauses Using Conjunctions

Now that we've established our clauses, we can introduce the matchmaker: conjunctions. These small words serve as the glue that holds clauses together to build longer sentences. "And" "but," "or," "for," "so," "however," and "nor" are the most commonly used.

- Independent Clause + Conjunction + Dependent Clause
- The cat chased the mouse (independent) because (conjunction) it was hungry (dependent).

Voila! A lovely, complete statement is formed.

1.4   Using Transitions to Connect Ideas

Transitions are the sentence's fairy godmothers. They facilitate the flow of your ideas and direct your reader (or listener) from one point to another. "But," "hence," "in addition," "on the other hand," and "meanwhile" are some common instances.

Example: The cat chased the mouse. *However,* it managed to escape.

- ❖ Remember, practice makes perfect, so don't be afraid to get creative and have fun with it!

Section 2: Tips for Effective English Communication

2.1 Active Listening: Showing Interest, Asking Questions, and Paraphrasing

Let's begin this subject by discussing active listening. Assume you're at a party (yes, those ancient social gatherings where humans used to interact face-to-face). You're having a conversation with someone and want them to feel respected and heard. You should express your interest, ask questions, and rephrase their statements. So, lean in, nod, and offer them your undivided attention. They'll appreciate it!

2.2 Clarity and Brevity: Keeping Your Message Simple and Concise

"Brevity is the spirit of wit," someone knowledgeable once said (probably). To put it another way, less is more. Keep your message brief and concise when talking in English. Eliminate jargon, extraneous details, and complicated sentence constructions. The easier it is to understand your message, the simpler it is.

Long, convoluted message: *Simplified message:*

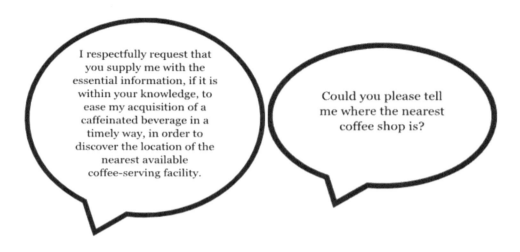

You tell me which one is better! Shorter one, right?

2.3 Tone and Politeness: Using Appropriate Language and Expressions for Various Situations

Whether you're speaking to your boss, a friend, or a stranger, it's critical to use the appropriate tone and vocabulary. Politeness is the secret sauce that makes every interaction run more smoothly. Understand when to use formal language and when to be more casual. Remember the golden rule: treat people as you would like to be treated.

Work (Colleague A and Colleague B):

Colleague A: "Excuse me, could you possibly spare a moment to help me with this report? I'm having trouble formatting the chart."

Colleague B: "Certainly, I'd be happy to assist you. Let's take a look at it together."

Friends (Friend A and Friend B):

Friend A: "Hey, do you mind if I borrow your phone charger for a bit? My battery is running low."

Friend B: "No problem at all! Here you go."

Strangers (Stranger A and Stranger B):

Stranger A: "Pardon me, I seem to be a bit lost. Would you be kind enough to direct me to the nearest bus stop?"

Stranger B: "Of course! You just need to head down this street, take a left at the corner, and you'll see it right there."

2.4 Non-verbal Communication: Body Language, Facial Expressions, and Gestures

Communication is an art form, and it's not just about the words you tie together - it's also about the silent strokes of creativity. Without saying a single word, your body language, facial expressions, and gestures may all tell a narrative. So, how about we paint a picture of confidence and friendliness?

To begin, stand tall and proud, as if you were the main character in a superhero film. This will demonstrate to people that you are at ease in your own skin and ready to engage in any topic. Keep eye contact, but not in a creepy, unblinking way. You want to connect with the person you're speaking with, not make them feel questioned by a secret agent.

Let us now discuss gestures. Maintain an open and friendly atmosphere. There's no need to behave like you're directing traffic at a busy intersection, but a few well-placed hand movements can assist underline your points and keep the conversation flowing.

Finally, don't underestimate the power of a smile. A genuine, pleasant grin can break the ice, build connections, and even brighten someone's day. It's like a free present that you may give to everyone you encounter if you brush your teeth first!

That's all there is to it. Learn the art of nonverbal communication, and you'll be a conversational Picasso in no time!

2.5 Overcoming Language Barriers: Using Synonyms, Rephrasing, and Simplifying Your Message

English is a tricky language, and you may need to overcome language difficulties at times. But don't worry! Utilizing synonyms, rephrasing, and simplifying your message can assist in closing the communication gap. And remember that patience is a virtue when in doubt.

- Ravi: "I am having trouble understanding some parts of this document."
- Linda: "Oh, do you mean the intricate nuances in this perplexing paper?"
- Ravi: "Sorry, I am not familiar with the words 'nuances' and 'perplexing.' Could you please explain?"
- Linda: "I apologize. I meant to say, do you mean the complicated details in this confusing paper?"
- Ravi: "Yes, exactly! The complex information in this paper is hard for me to grasp."

- Linda: "Let me try to simplify it for you: The paper has a lot of details that are difficult to understand."
- Ravi: "Ah, I see. Thank you for making it clearer!"

2.6 Practice Scenarios for Effective Communication

Let's put those abilities to use now that we've studied the fundamentals of good English communication! In the following examples, practice active listening, clarity, tone, non-verbal communication, and overcoming language hurdles.

Scenario 1: A Job Interview:

"So, tell me about your experience in this field," the interviewer asks.

Applicant: "I've worked in the sector for five years, focusing mostly on project management and team leadership. I've successfully managed a number of projects, completing them on schedule and under budget."

Scenario 2: Your first meeting with your partner's parents:

"Mom and Dad, here is Sam, my significant other."

Parent: "It's a pleasure to meet you, Sam. Please have a seat and make yourself at home."

Sam: "Thank you very much, Mr. and Mrs. Johnson. It's also a pleasure to meet you."

Scenario 3: Discussing a project with colleagues:

Colleague 1: "I think we should focus on strengthening our marketing efforts for this project,"

Colleague 2: "That's a fantastic concept. To entice more customers, we may also consider presenting a special incentive."

Colleague 3: "Yeah, I absolutely agree. Let's explore some ideas and develop a marketing strategy."

Section 3: Writing Tips and Tricks

3.1 Writing clear and coherent sentences:

Clarity is king in the world of writing. It is critical that your phrases deliver your intended message without ambiguity or uncertainty. Keep the following suggestions in mind when writing sentences:

a) Less is more: short sentences are your best friend. Keep to the point and avoid long-winded sentences that require you to take a deep breath to read aloud. Recall that a brief sentence is significantly more striking and understandable.

b) Use the right words: Using the right phrases allows you to effectively explain your ideas. Use words that are exact and distinct, and that truly describe your thoughts. A thesaurus is a useful tool but you should use it wisely: often basic words are more effective than their fancier counterparts.

c) Subject-verb agreement: Ensuring that your subjects and verbs agree is an important component of writing clear sentences. A plural subject necessitates a plural verb, whereas a solitary subject necessitates a singular verb. Keep an eye on this to avoid grammatical errors.

d) Active voice: Employing the active voice improves the engagement and directness of your phrases. While the passive voice has its uses, excessive use can result in a dull and monotonous writing style. Thus, use the active voice to bring your words to life!

e) Change up your sentence structure: Changing up your sentence structure keeps the reader interested. Mix simple, compound, and complicated sentences to create a smooth flow that keeps readers interested without overwhelming them.

f) Punctuation is important: Correct punctuation is necessary for clear communication. Commas, periods, and other punctuation marks assist readers in understanding your intended meaning and navigating your phrases. Employ them with caution, and avoid using too much punctuation, which may confuse your viewers.

By following these guidelines, you will be able to write clear and coherent sentences that will resonate with your readers, making your writing both memorable and successful.

3.2 Writing for different purposes:

Ah, the age-old dilemma of whether to wear a respectable top hat and monocle or casual flip-flops and informal slang. Context is everything when it comes to writing! Let's look at how to find the correct blend of formal and informal language based on the situation.

a) Formal writing: Imagine you're at a black-tie party, munching on canapés and sipping champagne. This is the written counterpart to formal writing. Whether writing a research paper, a professional report, or a job application, you should use a more formal tone. Here's how to improve your writing:

- ✓ Use a complex vocabulary, but don't go overboard. It's not a race to see who can use the most unusual words.
- ✓ Maintain the order and organization of your phrases. Now isn't the time for witty asides or run-on sentences.

✓ Employ proper punctuation and prevent contractions, which can appear too casual.

✓ Keep in mind your audience's expectations and any specific formatting or style rules.

b) Informal writing: Imagine you're relaxing on a beach, soaking in the rays and sipping a refreshing beverage. This is where informal writing can help. You can let loose and have some fun whether texting your buddies, writing a personal blog, or creating a clever social media post. To embrace your more casual side:

✓ Employ common jargon and slang, but don't go overboard to the point that your message becomes unintelligible.

✓ Feel free to break grammatical and punctuation standards as long as it doesn't interfere with comprehension.

✓ To make your writing more conversational, use contractions and abbreviations.

✓ Consider your audience and write to their tastes and interests.

Thus, whether you're sporting a top hat and monocle for a formal soirée or kicking back in your flip-flops for a casual seaside talk, remember to tailor your writing style to the occasion. This ensures that your message is not only well heard, but also perfectly fitted to the context in which it is presented.

Key Takeaways

- Writing and speaking in English are vital components of language acquisition and communication.
- Understanding sentence structure, including subject, verb, and object, as well as using conjunctions and transitions to connect ideas, is required for creating entire sentences.
- Active listening, clarity and brevity, tone and civility, nonverbal communication, and overcoming language difficulties are all components of effective communication.
- Practicing diverse communication scenarios increases confidence and adaptability in a variety of contexts.
- Effective written communication requires the ability to write clear and cohesive sentences, grasp paragraph structure, and modify language for varied purposes.
- Editing and proofreading your work will result in polished writing by improving grammar, punctuation, and spelling.
- Composing emails, letters, and short essays as practice exercises will help you develop your writing skills and become a more confident and competent communicator.

Writing Exercises

It's time to flex those writing muscles and show off your linguistic ability, word warriors! Workout 5 provides a delicious array of difficulties that will put your newly gained talents to the test, quickly transforming you into a wordsmith extraordinaire. Therefore, roll up your sleeves, grab your quill (or keyboard), and prepare to enter the exciting world of writing practice.

So, let's get started with some workout prompts that will challenge your readers to write interesting emails, letters, and short essays! Make sure to try these prompts and look at the answer key samples at the conclusion to see how they compare!

Prompts for Exercises:

- **Email:** Send an email to a coworker asking for feedback on a project idea. Include the project's objectives, timeframes, and any specific questions you have for them.

- **Letter:** Write a thank-you letter to your favorite high school teacher, expressing your appreciation for the influence they had on your life and providing an update on your current activities.

- **Short Essay:** In a 300-word essay, explore the value of successful workplace communication and offer three suggestions for improving communication among team members.

Answer Key Examples:

1. Email:

Subject: Request for Input on Project Proposal

Hi [Colleague's Name],

I hope you're doing well. I'm currently working on a project proposal for our next product launch and would greatly appreciate your advice. This project's primary objectives are to raise brand awareness and boost sales through targeted marketing initiatives.

The proposal is due on April 15th, and I would like your feedback by April 10th to allow for adjustments. I'm especially interested in your opinions on the following:

- Our target audience's most successful marketing routes.
- Ad expenditure optimization strategies.
- Measures for measuring campaign success.

Please contact me if you have any queries or need any extra information. I eagerly await your insightful comments.

Best wishes,

[Your Name]

2. Letter:

Dear [Name of Teacher],

I hope you are in excellent health and spirits as I write this letter. As a former student at [School Name], I'd like to offer my heartfelt appreciation for the vital lessons and guidance you provided during my time in your classroom.

Your enthusiasm for [topic] and commitment to the achievement of your students motivated me to work harder and strive for perfection. I am presently pursuing a degree in [field] at [university], and I credit a large portion of my academic and personal development to the foundation you helped establish throughout my high school years.

Thank you for leaving an indelible mark on my life and serving as an inspiration to me. I wish you continued success in your teaching profession and hope to cross paths with you again soon.

Best wishes,

[Your name]

3. Short Essay:

Effective communication is critical in the workplace because it promotes collaboration, builds relationships, and boosts productivity. Communication skills are more important than ever in an increasingly interconnected society. This paper will go through three ways for improving workplace communication among team members.

First and foremost, it is critical to foster an open dialogue culture. Encourage employees to communicate their thoughts, concerns, and feedback to build trust and respect. Regular team meetings, anonymous suggestion boxes, and open-door policies can help achieve this.

Second, giving precise and unambiguous instructions reduces misconceptions and ensures jobs are executed correctly and effectively. Managers should take the time to define their expectations and, when necessary, offer written documentation.

Finally, engaging in team-building activities can assist employees in developing stronger interpersonal relationships, which can lead to increased communication. These activities might range from volunteer projects to team meals and communication skills courses.

To summarize, firms may foster a workplace where effective communication thrives by encouraging open discourse, offering clear instructions, and engaging in team-building activities. This leads to higher productivity and overall success.

Wrapping It Up: The Conclusion to Your English Communication Journey

Congrats, pals! We've reached the end of our linguistic adventure, but the fun doesn't end there. As you continue to improve your English, remember that communicating is a journey that never ends. Therefore, why not seize life by the vowels and make each interaction memorable?

By putting the strategies, methods, and techniques we've discussed in this chapter into practice, you'll be well on your way to being a communication ace. You'll be able to handle any situation, from nailing that job interview to impressing your partner's parents.

So go on, my fellow wordsmiths, and let your inner Shakespeare (or Dr. Seuss) loose on the world. You can do it! And if you ever get stuck, remember that communication is all about connecting, so don't be afraid to exhibit some emotion.

Continue to practice, learn, and be your wonderful self. And as always, know that we're cheering you on from the sidelines. Good luck with your communication!

Chapter 10: Review and Practice

"Repetition is the mother of learning, the father of action, which makes it the architect of accomplishment."

- Zig Ziglar

Hello there, grammar experts! We've arrived at the end of our amazing adventure, but don't worry, we still have one more stop to make. That's right, it's time to go over everything we've studied and put it into practice so you can become the grammar master you were always intended to be. Believe us when we say that your future self will be grateful that you took this step toward long-term retention and mastery. Now, let's get started and work on those grammatical muscles one more time!

Grammar Review

Hold on to your grammar hats, because we're about to go on a grammar review trip down memory lane! We'll go over some of the most important building blocks of English language in this part. You know, the old-fashioned elements of speech that form the foundation of our language.

First and foremost, let us discuss **nouns,** the English language's robust little workhorses. Nouns are words that identify individuals, places, things, or concepts. They can be common or proper, singular or multiple, and used in many contexts. Look at the following sentences:

- This morning, I ate my <u>breakfast.</u>
- <u>Sally</u> dashed towards the <u>park.</u>
- <u>The book</u> on the shelf belongs to me.

Nouns in these lines include "breakfast," "Sally," "park," and "book." They each refer to a certain product, person, or location. Isn't it simple? I know you remember!

Following that are **verbs,** which are the engines that propel our sentences onward. Verbs are action words that describe what the sentence's subject is doing or being. They can be basic or complicated, active, or passive, and employed in a variety of tenses to show when an action is taking place. As an example:

- Every day, she <u>walks</u> to school.
- The sun is out and <u>blazing</u> beautifully.
- They'll <u>arrive</u> shortly.

"Walks," "blazing," and "arrive" are all verbs in these lines. They each depict what the individual is doing, is, or will do in the future.

Let's talk about **adjectives**, the colorful tiny paint brushes of the English language. Adjectives are words that describe or alter nouns. They can be used to denote size, color, shape, or any number of other characteristics. For instance:

- The <u>large red</u> balloon floated away.
- I noticed a <u>lovely, fluffy</u> kitty.
- She arrived at the party wearing a <u>beautiful blue</u> gown.

"Large," "red," "lovely," "fluffy," "beautiful," and "blue" are all adjectives in these lines. They each describe or modify a noun in some way, making the sentences more detailed and fascinating.

Sentence formation entails putting together building components to form sentences. **Simple, compound, and complicated sentences** are the three primary forms of sentences. Simple sentences include one independent clause, compound sentences have two or more independent clauses linked together by a coordinating conjunction, and complex sentences have one independent clause and at least one dependent clause.

- Simple: The dog barked at the mailman.
- Compound: The cat chased the mouse, but it got away.
- Complex: After I finish my homework, I'm going to the movies.

In these sentences, the first one is a simple sentence because it contains only one independent clause ("the dog barked at the mailman"). The second sentence is a compound sentence because it contains two independent clauses joined by the coordinating conjunction "but" ("the cat chased the mouse" and "it got away"). The third sentence is a complex sentence because it contains one independent clause ("I'm going to the movies") and one dependent clause ("after I finish my homework").

Here's a quick rundown of the 12 English verb tenses, along with a chart:

- **Simple Present Tense:** Used to describe habitual actions or general truths.
- Present Continuous/Progressive Tense: Used to describe actions that are happening now.

- o **Present Perfect Tense:** Used to describe actions that started in the past and continue to the present.
- o **Present Perfect Continuous/Progressive Tense:** Used to describe actions that started in the past and continue up to the present with an emphasis on the duration of the action.
- o **Simple Past Tense:** Used to describe completed actions in the past.
- o **Past Continuous/Progressive Tense:** Used to describe ongoing actions in the past.
- o **Past Perfect Tense:** Used to describe actions that happened before another action in the past.
- o **Past Perfect Continuous/Progressive Tense:** Used to describe actions that happened before another action in the past and continued up to that action.
- o **Simple Future Tense:** Used to make predictions or discuss future events.
- o **Future Continuous/Progressive Tense:** Used to describe ongoing actions that will occur in the future.
- o **Future Perfect Tense:** Used to describe actions that will be completed by a certain point in the future.
- o **Future Perfect Continuous/Progressive Tense:** Used to describe actions that will be ongoing up to a certain point in the future.

Tense	Structure
Simple Present	Subject + Base Verb
Present Continuous	Subject + "to be" + Present Participle
Present Perfect	Subject + "have/has" + Past Participle

Present Perfect Continuous	Subject + "have/has" + been + Present Part.
Simple Past	Subject + Past Verb
Past Continuous	Subject + "was/were" + Present Participle
Past Perfect	Subject + "had" + Past Participle
Past Perfect Cont.	Subject + "had" + been + Present Participle
Simple Future	Subject + "will" + Base Verb
Future Continuous	Subject + "will" + be + Present Participle
Future Perfect	Subject + "will" + have + Past Participle
Future Perfect Cont.	Subject + "will" + have + been + Pres. Part.

I hope this helps!

It's now time to wade into the dark waters of gerunds and infinitives! Don't worry, we'll do our best to make this as easy as possible.

To begin, what are gerunds and infinitives? There are two sorts of verb forms that can serve in a phrase as nouns or adverbs. Gerunds are made by adding "-ing" to a verb (for example, "swimming," "running," "dancing"), whereas infinitives are the root form of a verb (e.g., "to swim," "to run," "to dance").

Gerunds and infinitives can be employed in a variety of contexts, including:

- o As the subject of a sentence: "Running is good exercise."
- o As the object of a verb: "I enjoy swimming in the ocean."
- o As the object of a preposition: "He is afraid of flying."
- o As the complement of a linking verb: "Her favorite hobby is dancing."

Let's now talk about punctuation and capitalization. These two aspects may appear to be unimportant afterthoughts but trust us when we say they may make or break your writing.

Some important punctuation and capitalization rules to remember are:

- o Periods are used to end declarative sentences or abbreviations (e.g. "Mr.," "Dr.")
- o Commas are used to divide items in a list, to separate introductory sentences, and to signify pauses in speech or writing.
- o Apostrophes: used to show possession or contraction (for example, "Bob's car" or "it's raining").
- o Capital letters are used to begin a new sentence, to begin a proper noun (for example, "New York City"), or to emphasize an important word or phrase.

So, there you have it, everyone! Although gerunds, infinitives, punctuation, and capitalization are not the most exciting things in the world, mastering them can make a significant impact on your writing and communication skills. So go forth and defeat those pesky grammar gremlins!

Conceptual Exercises:

1. Identify the parts of speech in the following sentence:

"The quick brown fox jumped over the lazy dog."

2. Choose the correct verb tense to complete the following sentence: "I _____ my breakfast an hour ago."
   a) ate
   b) eat
   c) will eat
   d) eating
3. Create a complex sentence using a dependent clause.

Application Exercises:

1. Write a persuasive email to your boss using modal verbs to request a raise.
2. Create a sentence using passive voice.
3. Write a short paragraph describing a memorable experience using past and present tenses.

Answer Key

Conceptual exercises:

1. Noun: fox, dog
   Adjective: quick, brown, lazy
   Verb: jumped
   Preposition: over
   Article: the
   Conjunction: and
   Pronoun: none

2. a) ate

3. After I finish my work, I will go for a run.

Application exercises:

1. The answer may vary, but should use modal verbs such as "could," "should," or "would" to politely request a raise.
2. The cake was baked by Lyn.
3. A trip to Hawaii with my family last summer was a remarkable experience for me. We went to gorgeous beaches, hiked to a waterfall, and tried different foods. One of my greatest memories is going snorkeling and seeing a variety of colorful fish and sea turtles. It was a once-in-a-lifetime opportunity that I will never forget. When I think back on that vacation, I am grateful for the time I spent with my family as well as the chance to explore a new place.

Chapter 11: Bonus Chapter: Common English Mistakes and How to Avoid Them

"The only real mistake is the one from which we learn nothing."
- Henry Ford

Oh, look who's back for some more English language fun! Congratulations if you're reading this! You've made it to the bonus round, where we'll take a deeper look at some of the most typical English learning mistakes. So don't worry, we're not here to make you feel bad about your mistakes. Instead, we'll give you the lowdown on how to avoid these errors like an expert.

In case you missed it, we took a trip down grammar lane in the last chapter and covered everything from nouns to verb tenses. It was a wild voyage, and we're so proud of you for surviving it. We're now taking things a step further by addressing those irritating errors that seem to creep into our writing and speech without warning.

So, buckle up, buttercup, and prepare to enter the world of typical English blunders. We're here to help you dodge them like a pro and improve your communication abilities. Let's get started!

Common Grammar Mistakes

So, let's get into the specifics of typical language errors, but don't worry, we're not here to pass judgment! We all make mistakes, which is completely fine. Yet, as the great philosopher Yoda famously said,

"The greatest teacher, failure is." Therefore, let us embrace our errors and learn from them!

• Subject-verb agreement errors: This mistake occurs when the subject and verb in a sentence don't match in terms of number (singular or plural). For example:

Incorrect: The group of students was late.

Correct: The group of students were late.

In this example, "group" is a singular noun, but "students" is plural. The correct verb form to use would be "were" to match the plural noun.

• Pronoun misuse and confusion: This mistake occurs when a pronoun is used incorrectly or is unclear in its referent. For example:

Incorrect: Jane and her ran to the store.

Correct: Jane and she ran to the store.

In this example, "her" is the incorrect pronoun to use. The correct pronoun to use would be "she," which matches the subject of the sentence.

• Misuse of prepositions: This mistake occurs when a preposition is used incorrectly or in the wrong place in a sentence. For example:

  o   Incorrect: I'm going to the store with.
  o   Correct: I'm going to the store with my friend.

In this example, the preposition "with" is used incorrectly. It needs to be followed by an object (my friend) to complete the sentence.

- Confusion between adjectives and adverbs: This mistake occurs when an adjective is used instead of an adverb or vice versa. For example:

  o Incorrect: He sings good.
  o Correct: He sings well.

In this example, "good" is an adjective, but "well" is an adverb. In this context, "well" is the correct word to use to modify the verb "sings."

- Mistakes in verb tense usage: This mistake occurs when the wrong verb tense is used in a sentence. For example:

  o Incorrect: I went to the store yesterday and buy some milk.
  o Correct: I went to the store yesterday and bought some milk.

In this example, the incorrect verb tense is used for the second verb in the sentence. The correct tense would be "bought" to match the past tense of the first verb.

! Remember, making mistakes is a natural part of the learning process, and it's okay to make them! By recognizing and avoiding common grammar mistakes, you'll become a more effective communicator and gain confidence in your English language skills.

Vocabulary Mistakes

Buckle up, guys, because we're about to enter the wild world of lexical errors! Even the most seasoned language learners can make these bothersome little mistakes, so don't feel guilty if you've made a few of your own. Let's look at a few of the most popular ones.

- There are many words in English that have similar sounds or appearances but different meanings. They are simple to conflate, yet doing so can result in some rather absurd (or embarrassing) mistakes. Examples of frequently misunderstood word pairings include "complement" and "complement," "accept" and "except," "affect" and "effect," and "advise" and "advice." Ensure you understand the distinction between them otherwise, you risk congratulating someone on their superb excepting abilities!

- Idiom and phrasal verb misuse: Idioms and phrasal verbs can be challenging to utilize since their meanings frequently diverge from the literal interpretations of the constituent terms. When someone says, "I'm feeling under the weather," they don't necessarily indicate that they are in the path of a storm. They are expressing their sickness. In a similar vein, if someone encourages you to "hang in there," they don't mean for you to grab a rope and hang there. They intend to stay strong in a trying circumstance. Make sure you grasp the meaning of idioms and phrasal verbs before employing them because using them incorrectly can result in muddled talks.

- Sentences with the wrong word order: Word order in English can be a little confusing, especially for non-native speakers. The meaning of a statement can occasionally be substantially altered by rearrangement of the words. For instance, "I only drink coffee in the morning" and "Only I drink coffee in the morning" have different meanings. When in doubt regarding word placement, it's best to err on the side of caution and choose a simple, uncomplicated sentence structure.

- Spelling mistakes and typos: Let's face it, even the best among us make mistakes occasionally. But they can be a big pain in the neck when it comes to writing. Your work may be difficult to comprehend if you misspell a word or use an incorrect homophone (a word that sounds similar but has a different meaning, such as "their" and "their"). Make sure to carefully edit your work or have someone else do it for you. Don't be hesitant to use a dictionary or spell-checker if you're having trouble spelling something.

You have it then, everyone! A little journey into the strange world of linguistic mistakes. Remember that learning involves making mistakes, so don't be too hard on yourself if you do. Who knows after all, right? You might even pick up a few new idioms in the process!

The End of an English Adventure: A Conclusion to Our Grammar Journey

Grab a cup of tea and get ready for a trip down memory lane because this Learn English Grammar Workbook for Adult Beginners is coming to an end.

The basics of English grammar, the subtleties of verb tenses, gerunds, and infinitives, as well as typical mistakes to avoid, have all been discussed in detail. We've laughed a bit, traded some puns, and maybe made learning English a little less scary and more enjoyable.

As you finish this book and continue on with your English learning journey, we want you to know that we are proud of you. Even as an adult, it takes a lot of guts to begin learning a new language, but you did it! You invested the necessary time, energy, and intelligence, and the results were an entirely new set of linguistic abilities.

A language acquisition process is a marathon, not a sprint, so keep that in mind. It takes time, practice, and patience to become proficient in any skill, especially one as challenging as English. So, don't be too hard on yourself if you don't do everything right the first time, or even the hundredth time. Every error is a chance for you to improve, and you're already lightyears ahead of where you were when you first started reading this book.

Speaking of chances, we're happy to inform you that this is just the beginning of your English language journey. Two more books in this series are available, and each one expands on the abilities and information you have already learned. Wait until you see what's in store for you in the next two books if you thought this one was fun and educational.

But let's take a moment right now to appreciate how far you've come. You now understand English grammar, can communicate more effectively, and are avoiding typical blunders. We can't wait to see what you accomplish next because you're already well on your way to being an English genius.

So, dear learner, go on and continue to learn. Continue to practice, continue to make mistakes, and continue to progress. The world is your oyster, and you can accomplish anything with your increased English skills.

Thank you for coming along for the adventure; we'll see you in the next book!

Made in the USA
Thornton, CO
10/22/23 07:23:16